# Cat Cam

## THE WORLD OF COOPER THE PHOTOGRAPHER CAT®

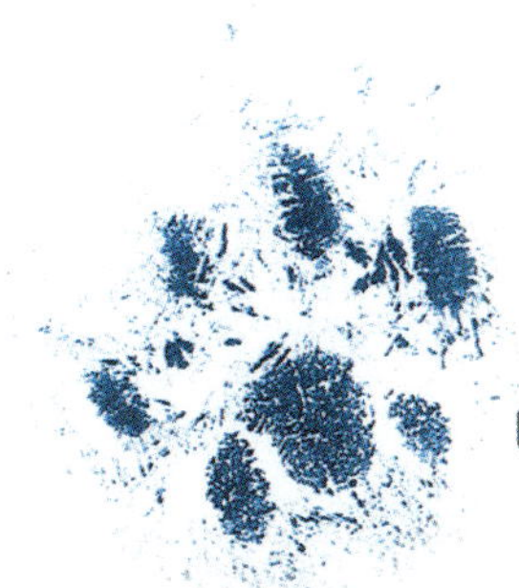

COOPER, MICHAEL AND DEIRDRE CROSS

Cat Cam: The World of Cooper the Photographer Cat ®



Cover design and front cover photo by Michael Cross. Logo by Ian Lynam.
Back cover photo by Kevin Law - Urban Light Studios.

First Edition
ISBN 978-0-615-41043-2

Printed in the United States of America

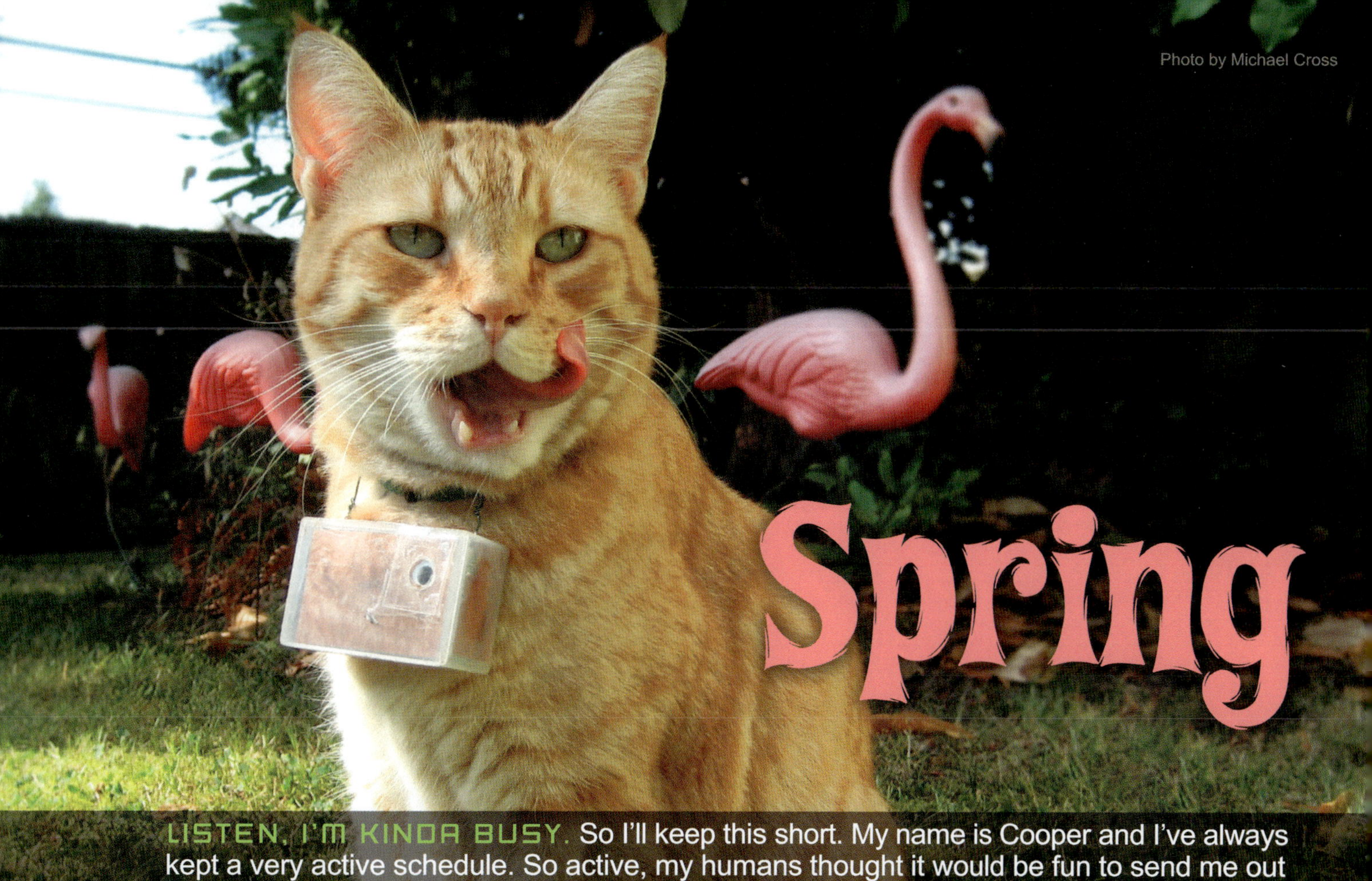


# Spring

LISTEN, I'M KINDA BUSY. So I'll keep this short. My name is Cooper and I've always kept a very active schedule. So active, my humans thought it would be fun to send me out once a week with a small digital camera on my collar to find out what I'm up to. So now I'm not only the neighborhood watch, it seems I am a documentary photographer, too. It's cool – the Cat Cam is light so I don't really notice it. I also find that the local lady cats rather dig a bad boy with a camera.

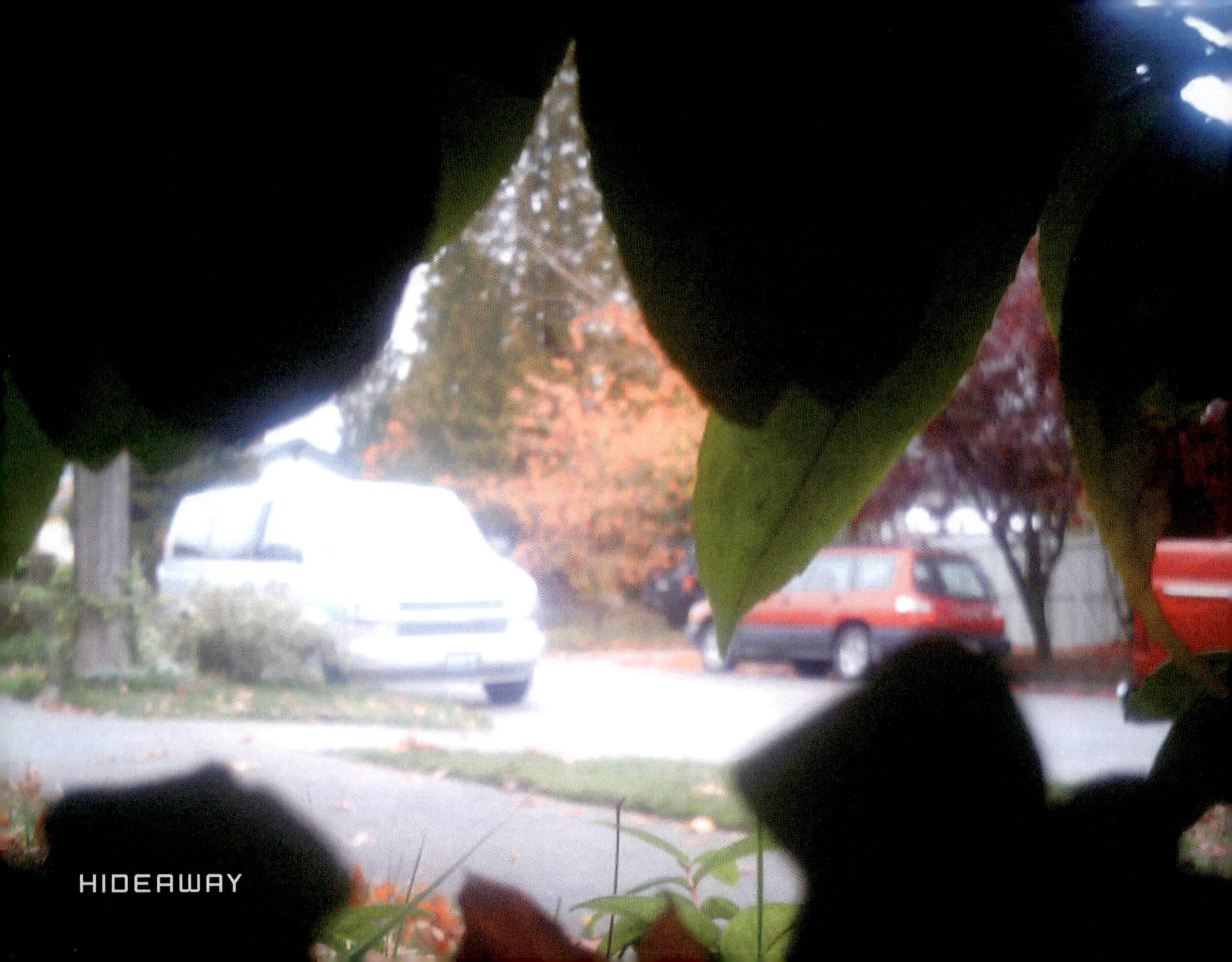
HIDEAWAY

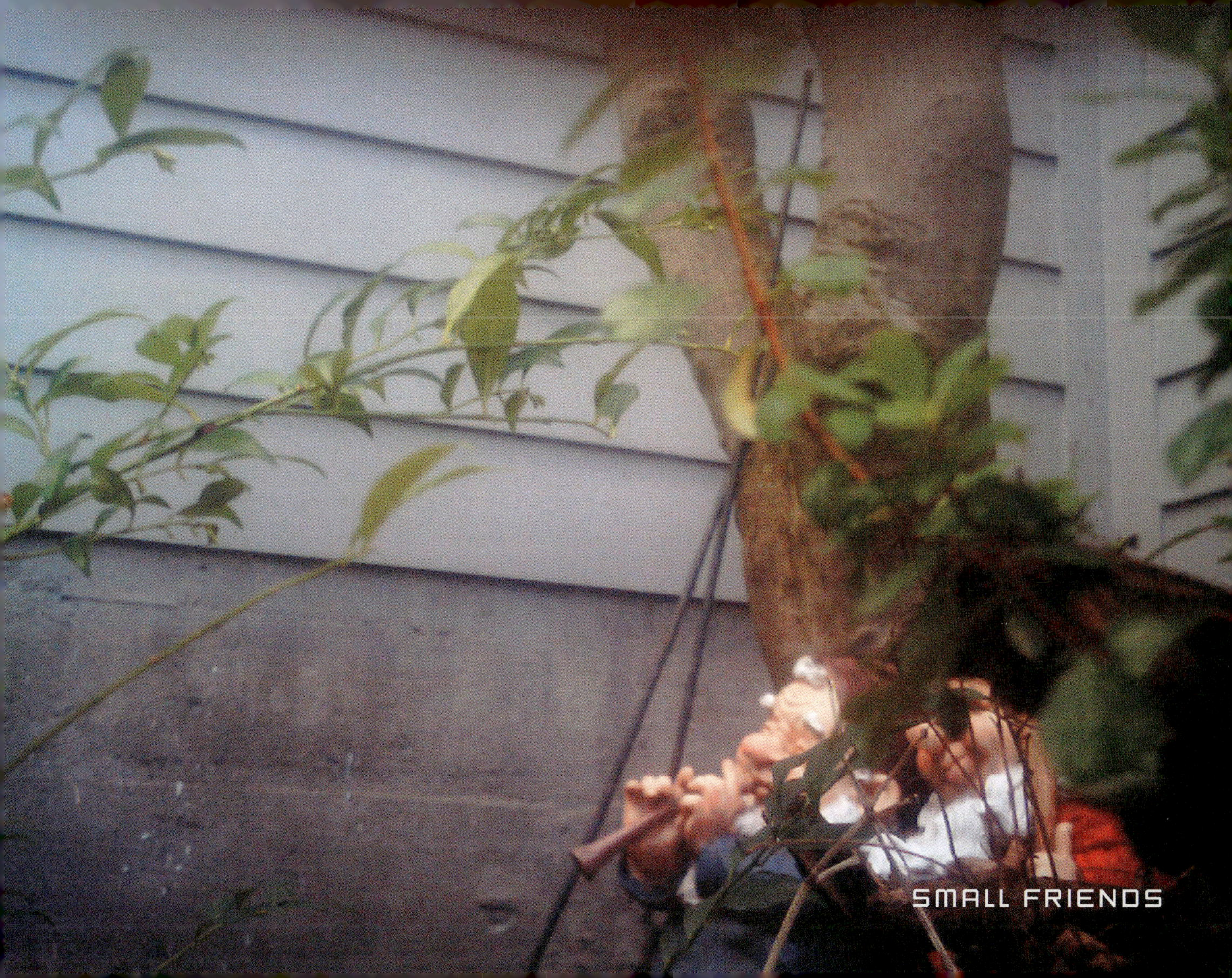
SMALL FRIENDS

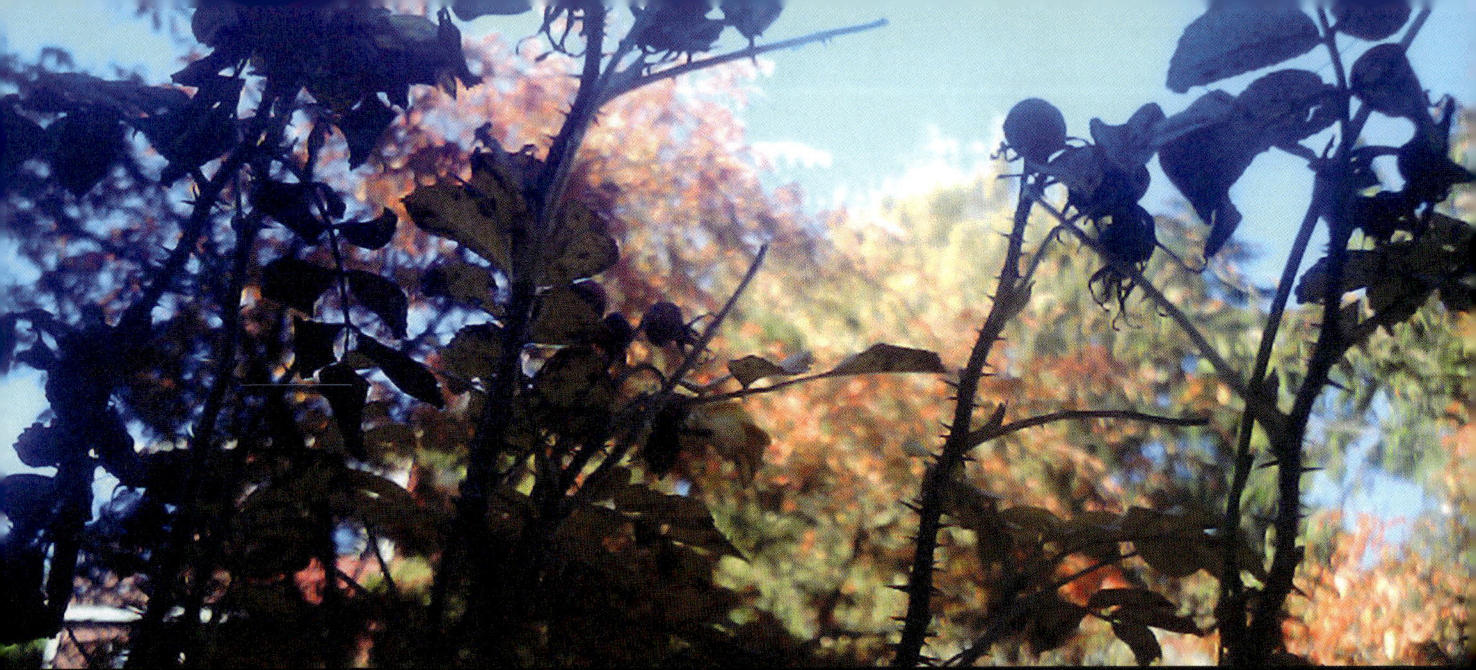

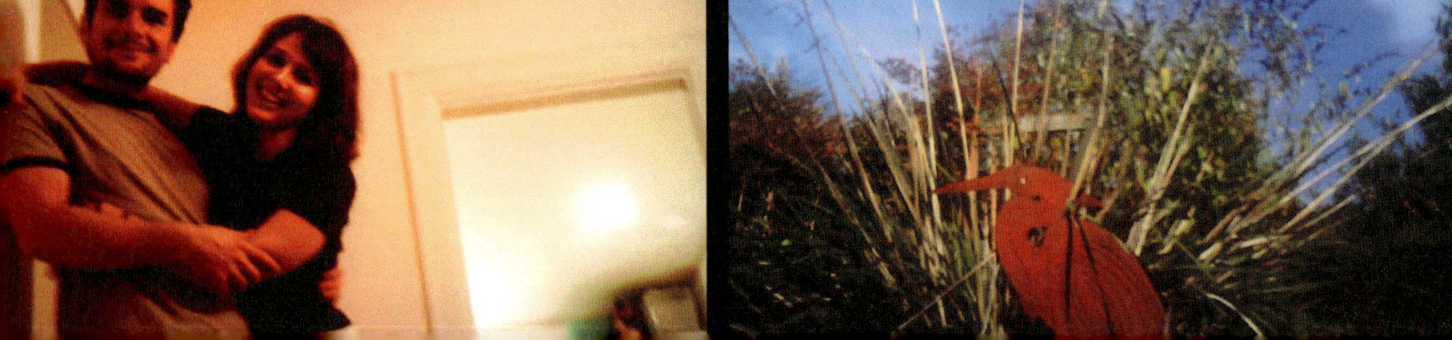

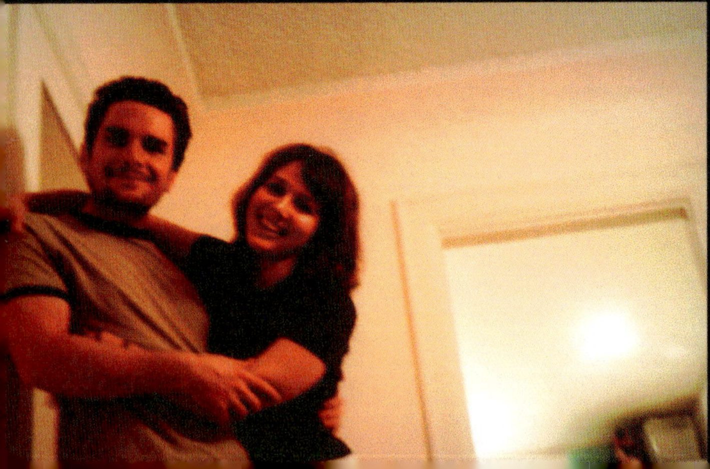

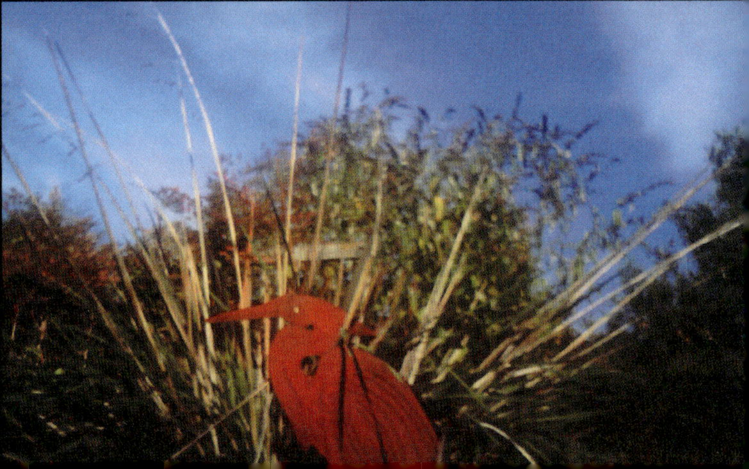

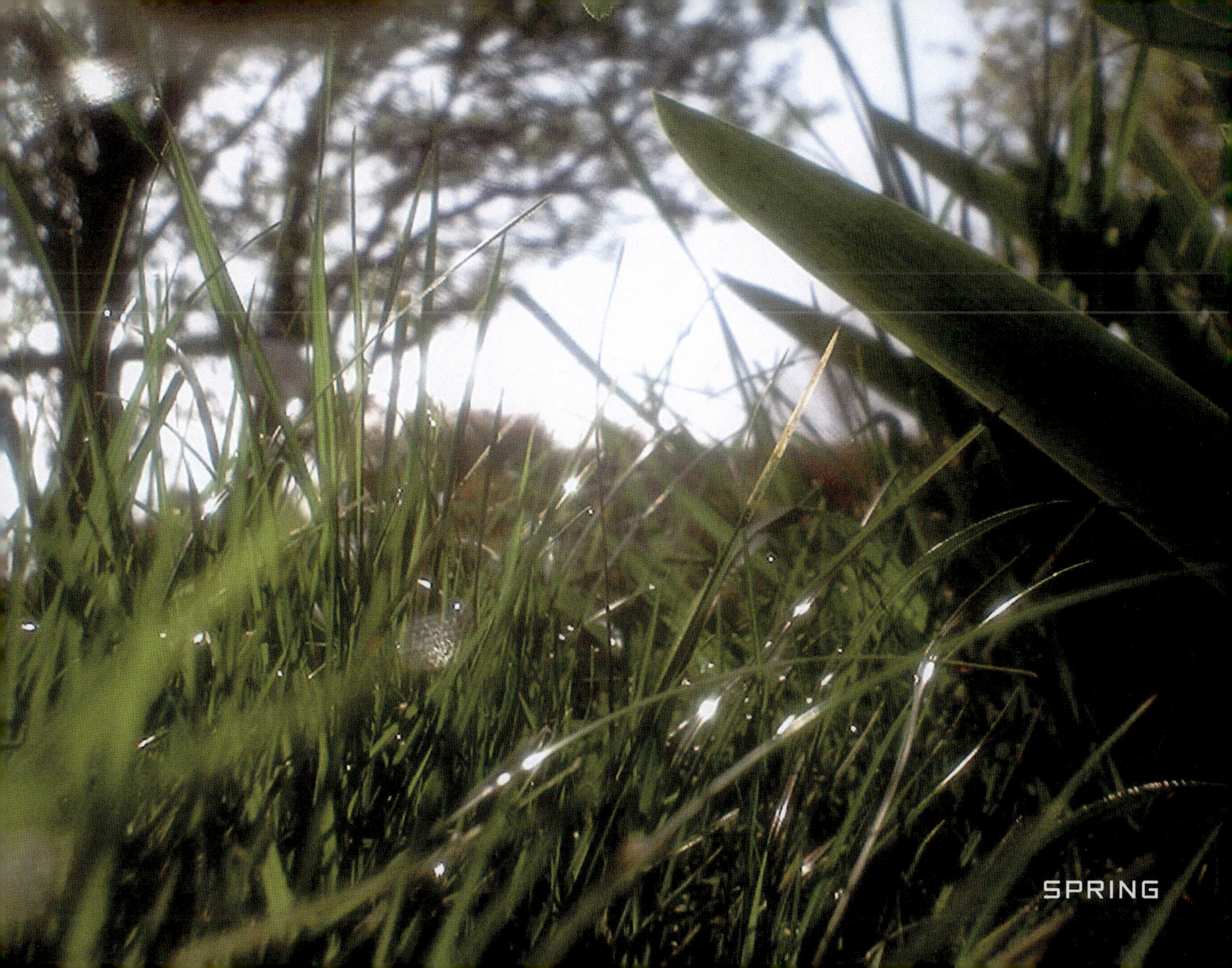
SPRING

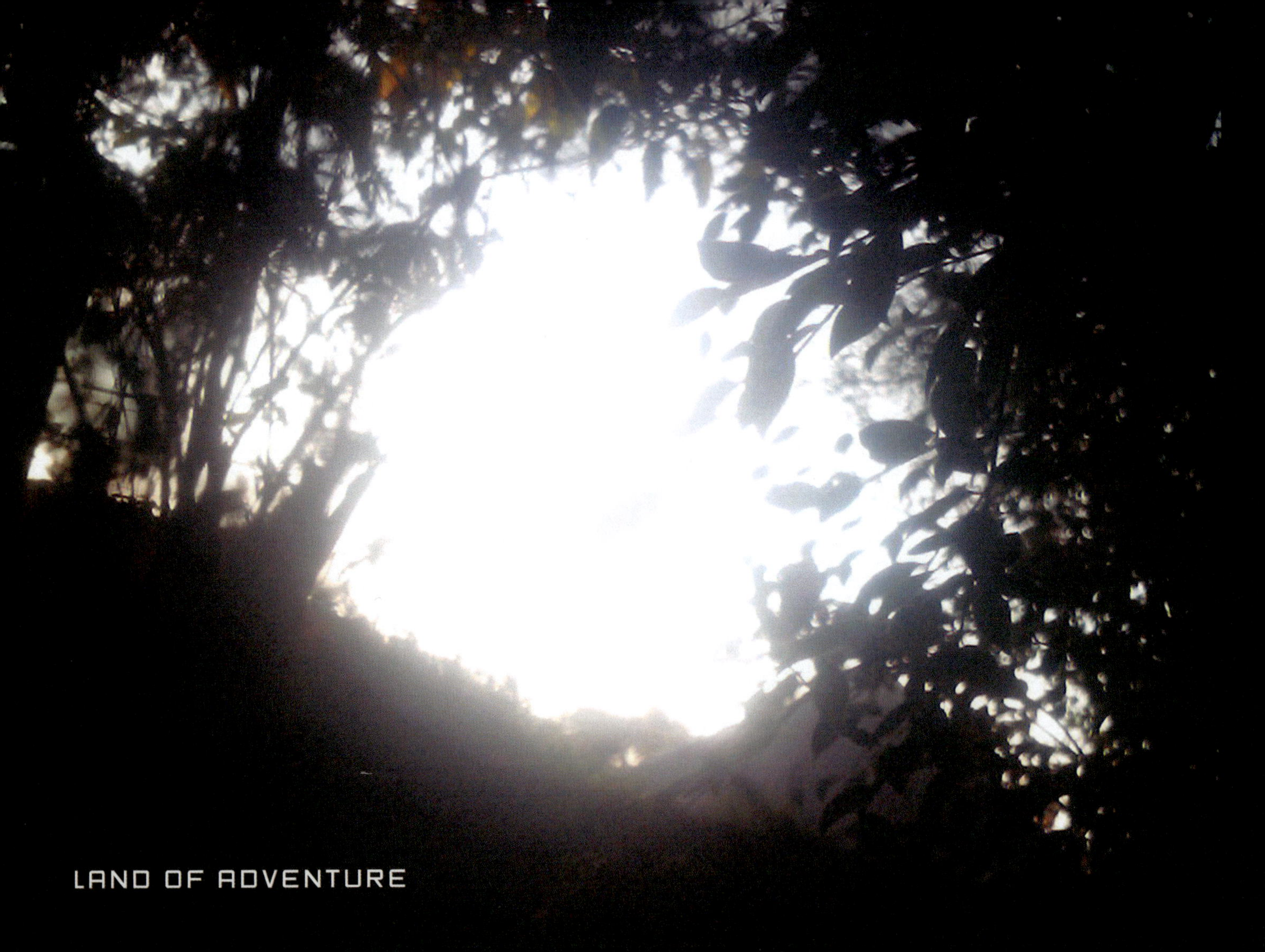
LAND OF ADVENTURE

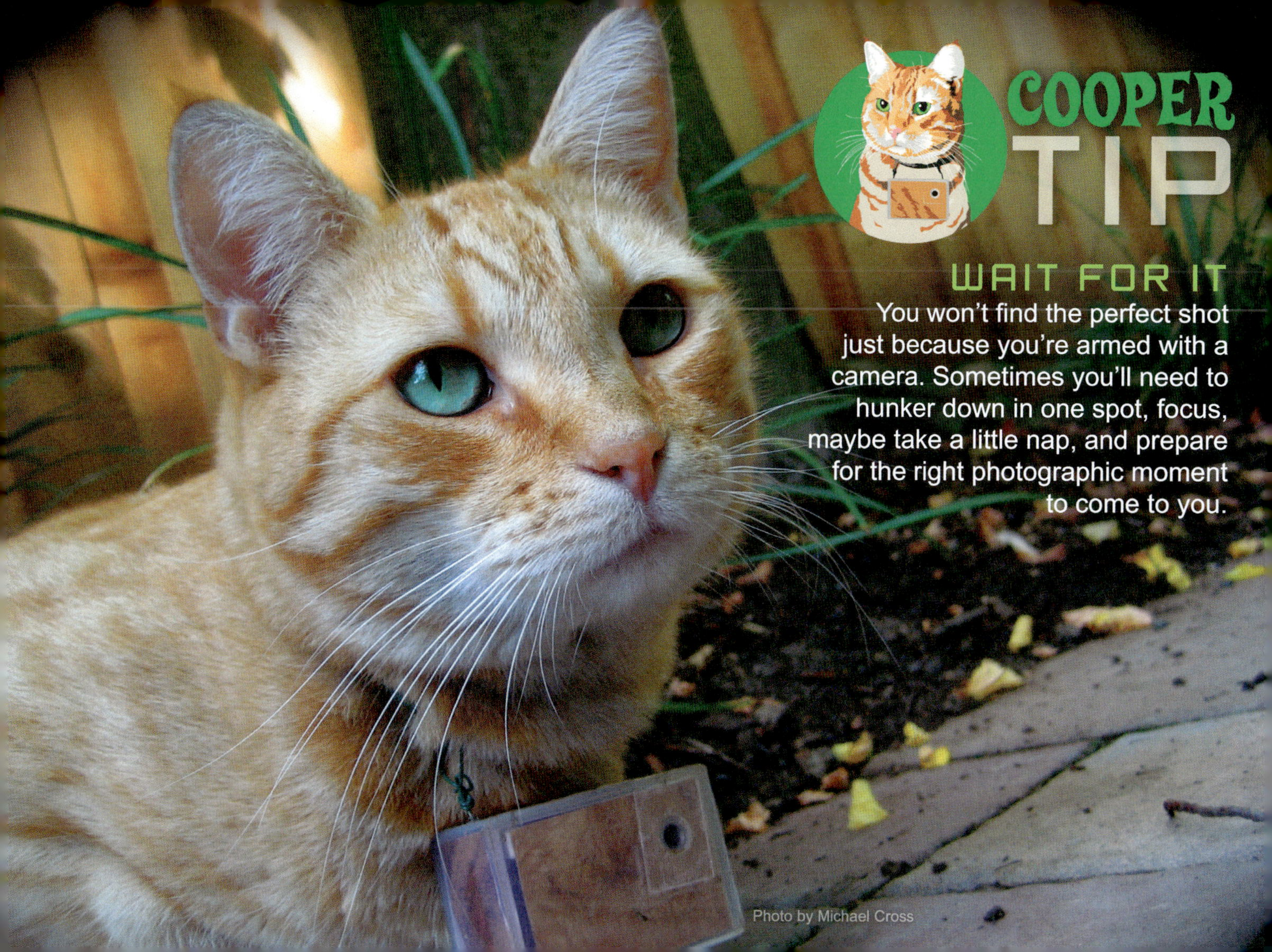
COOPER
TIP
WAIT FOR IT
You won't find the perfect shot just because you're armed with a camera. Sometimes you'll need to hunker down in one spot, focus, maybe take a little nap, and prepare for the right photographic moment to come to you.
Photo by Michael Cross

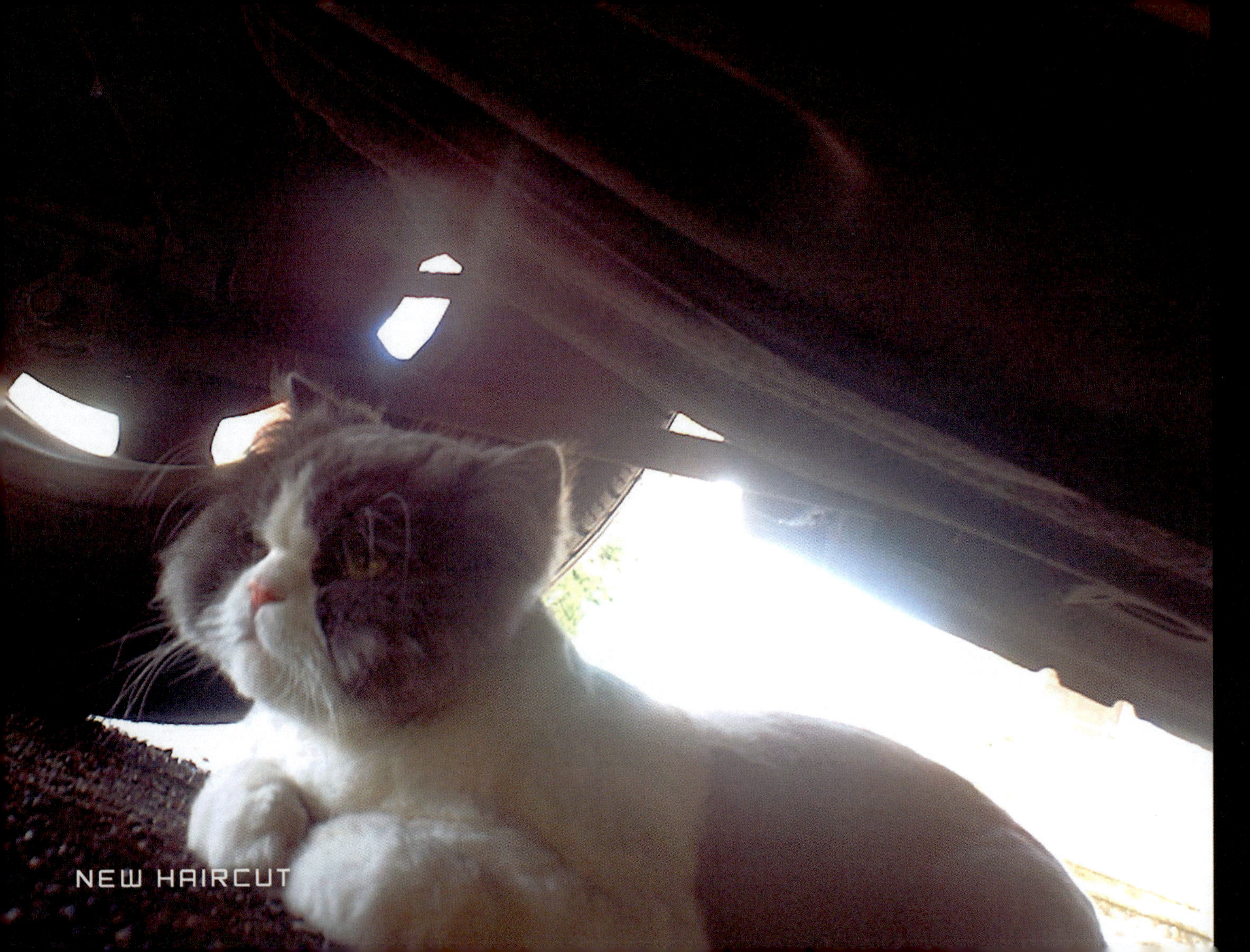
NEW HAIRCUT

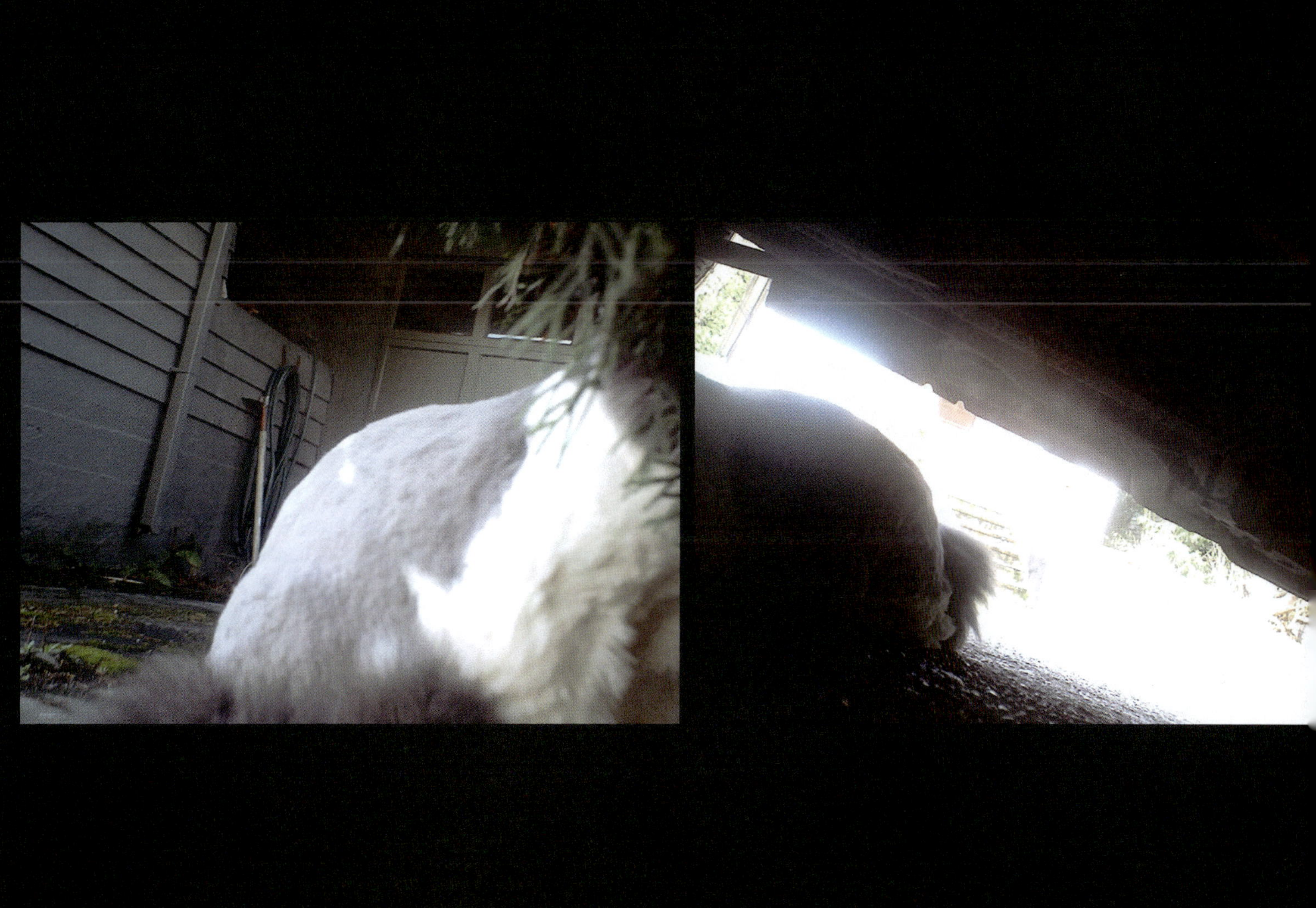

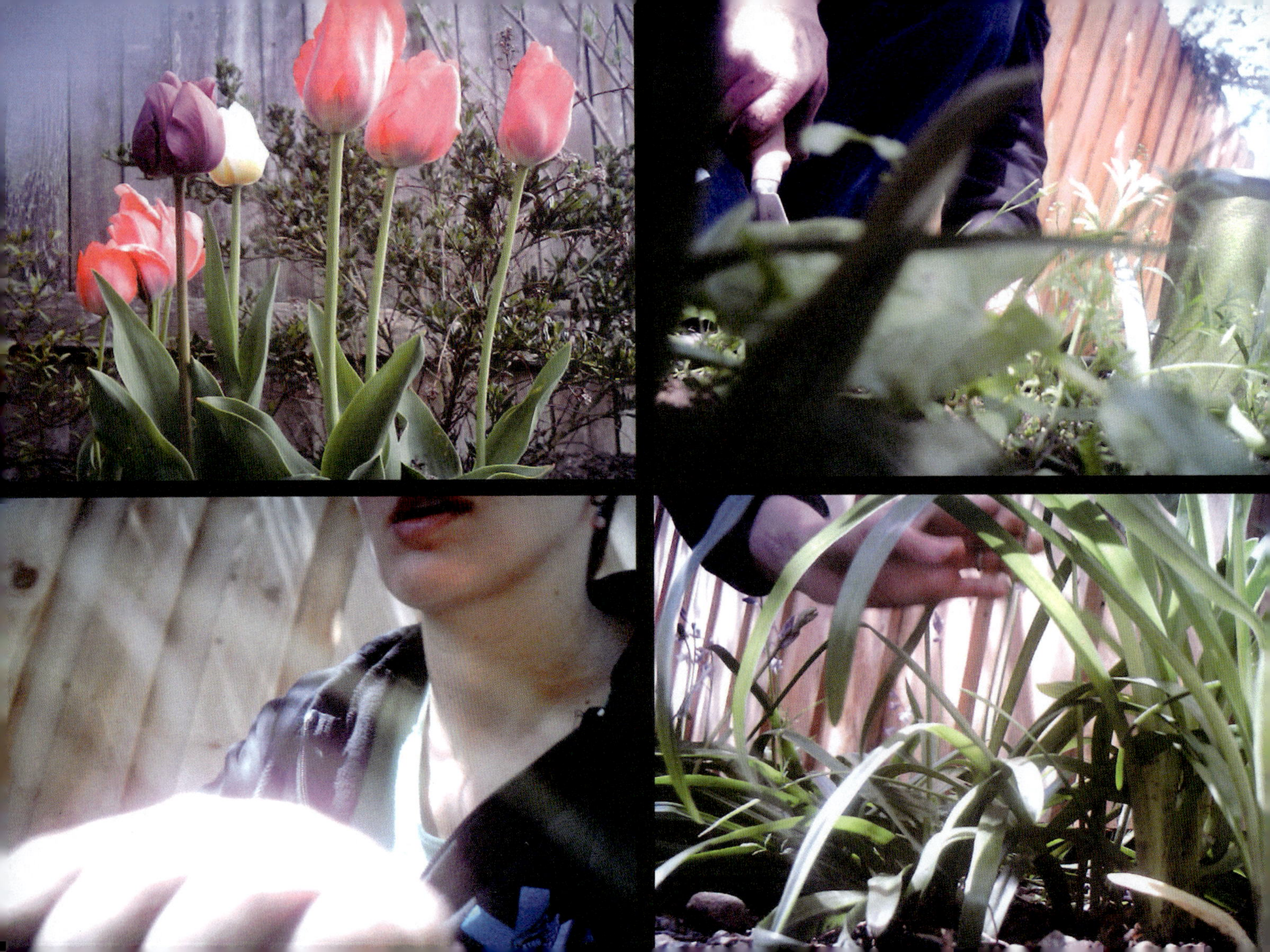

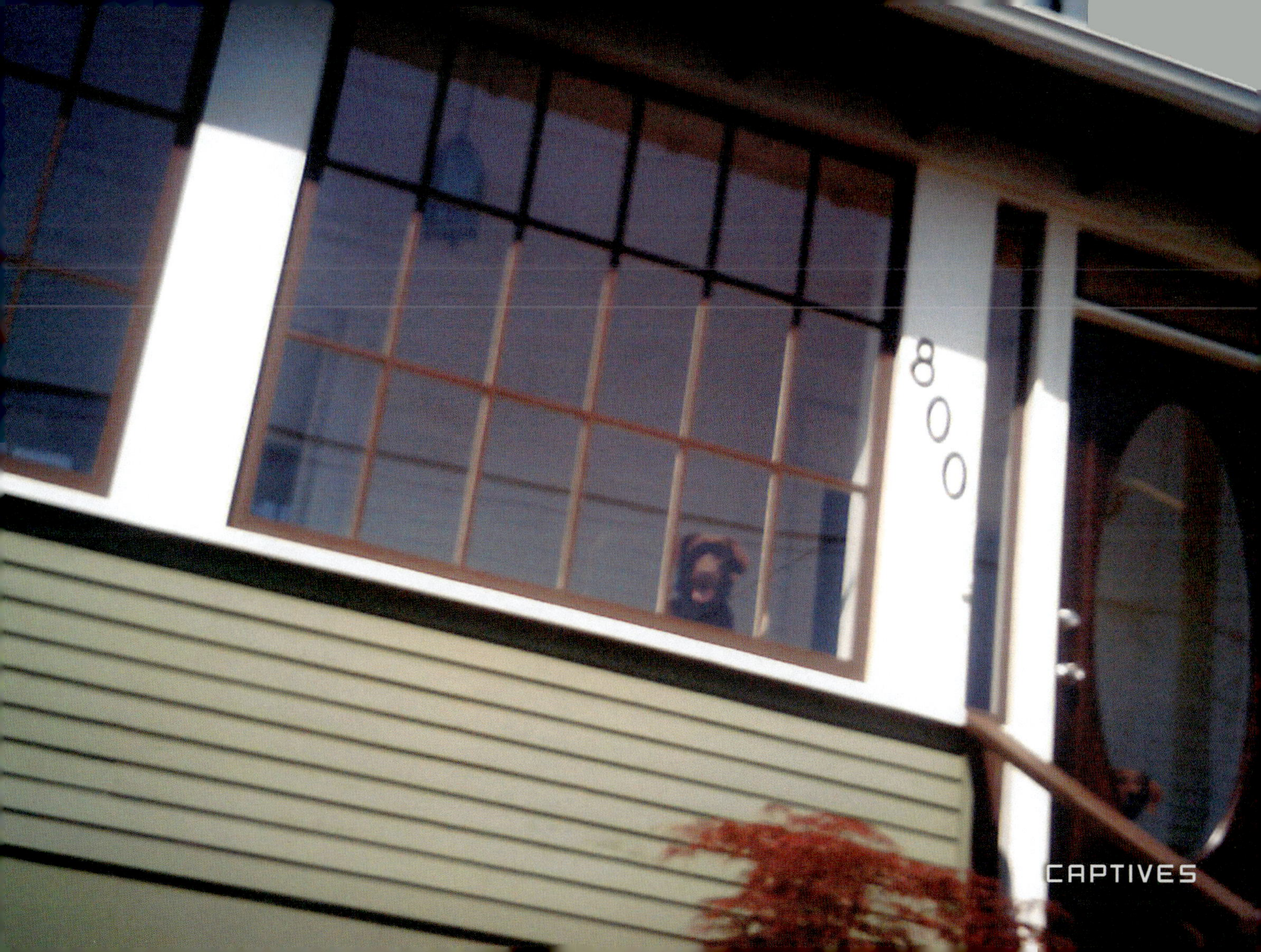


CAPTIVES

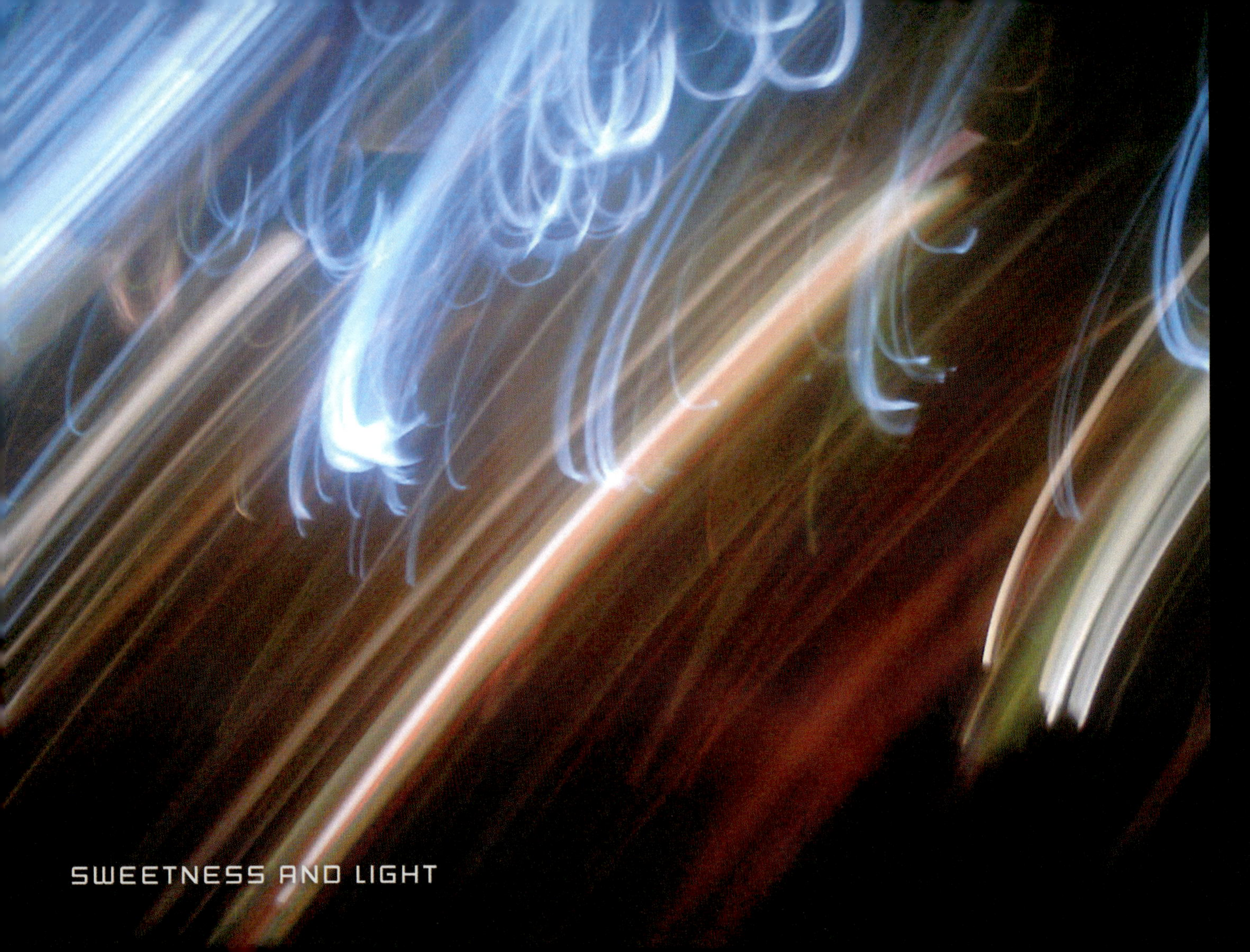
SWEETNESS AND LIGHT

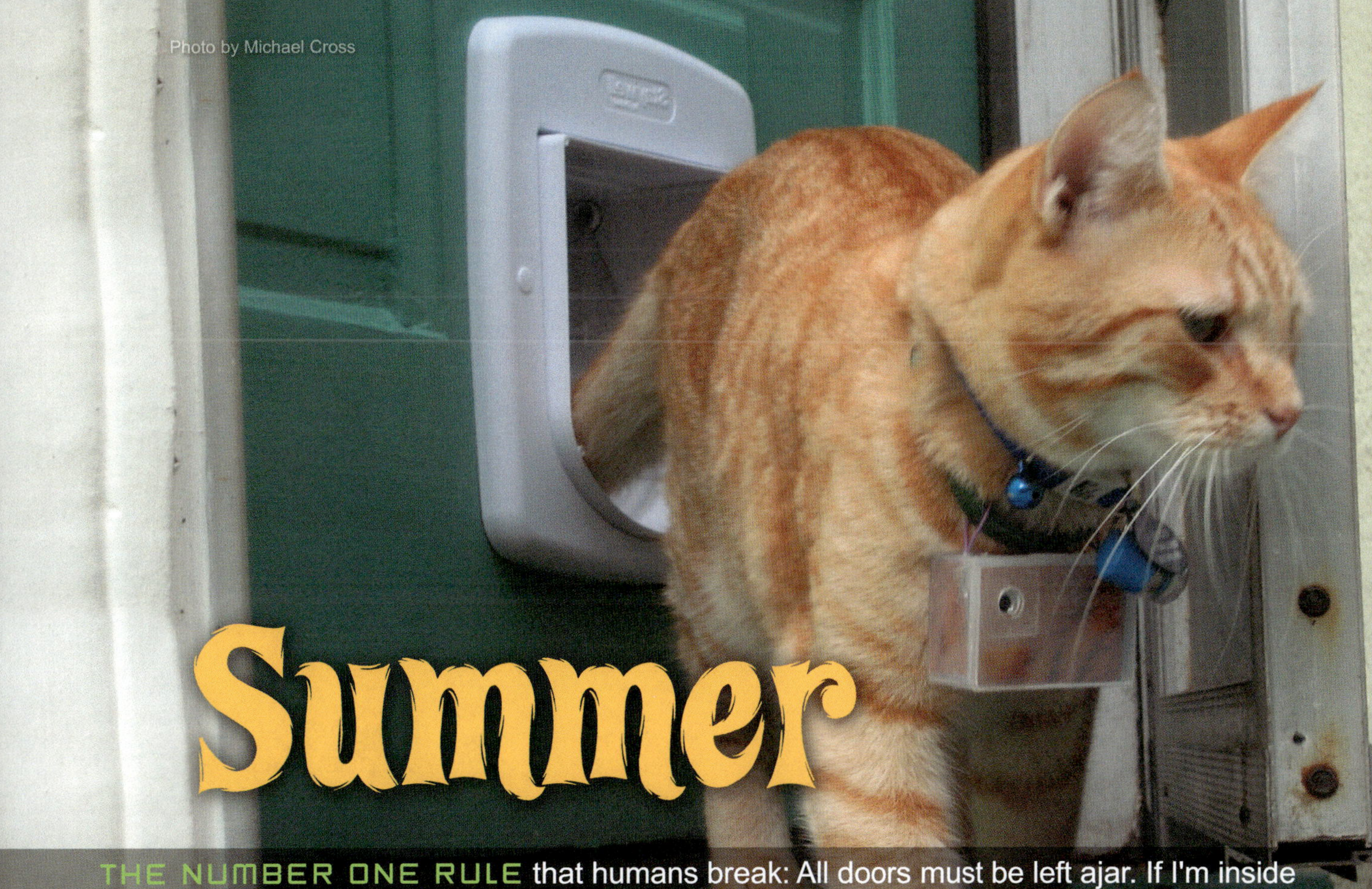


# Summer

THE NUMBER ONE RULE that humans break: All doors must be left ajar. If I'm inside I want outside. If I'm out I want in. This was the first important thing my humans learned about me through my photos, as I took a huge number of pictures while waiting at the door. So... genius - they installed a cat door for me! Just in time for summer parties, too. I'm still locked inside at night, but during the day I get to come and go as I please. Best of all, I get my artistic freedom!

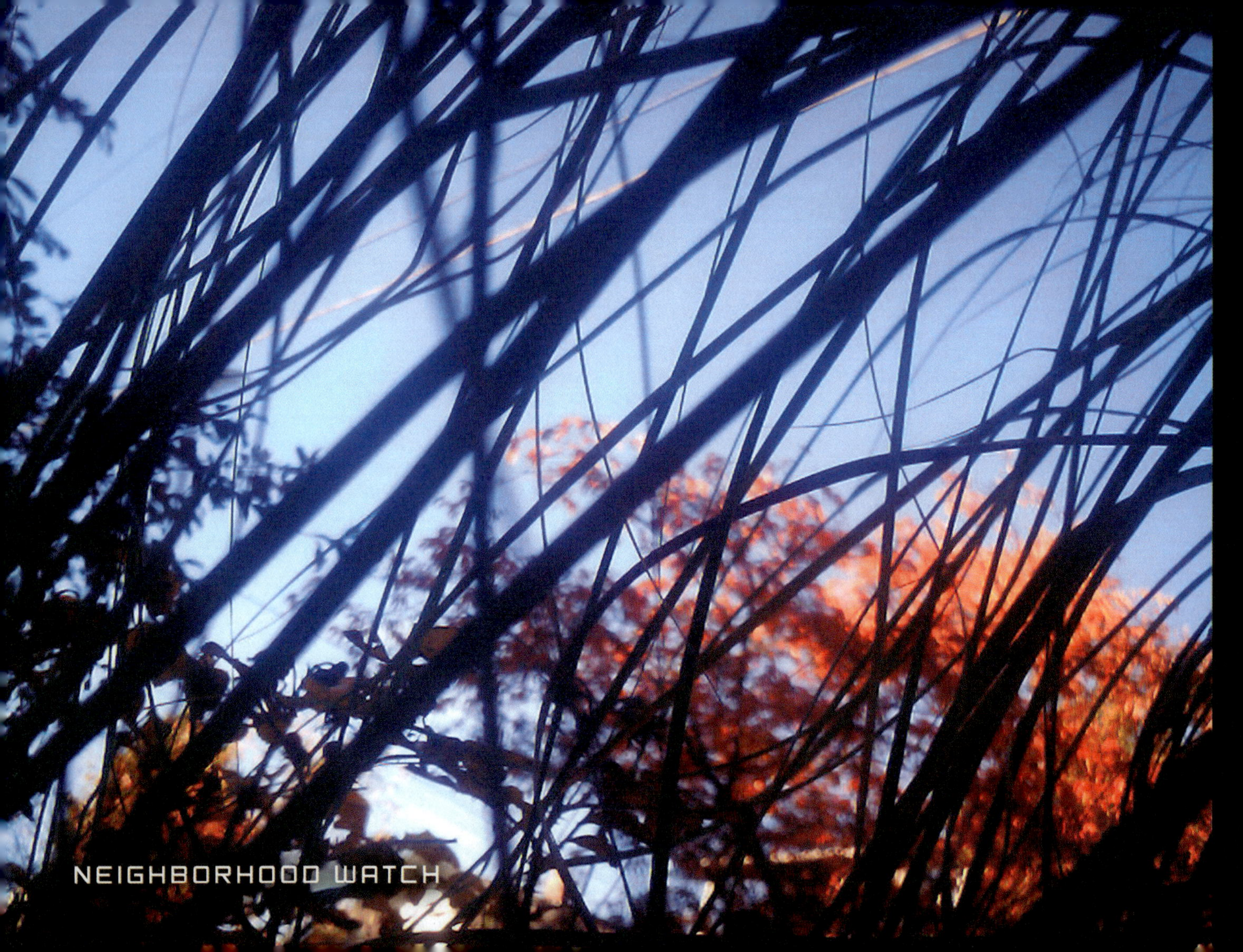
NEIGHBORHOOD WATCH

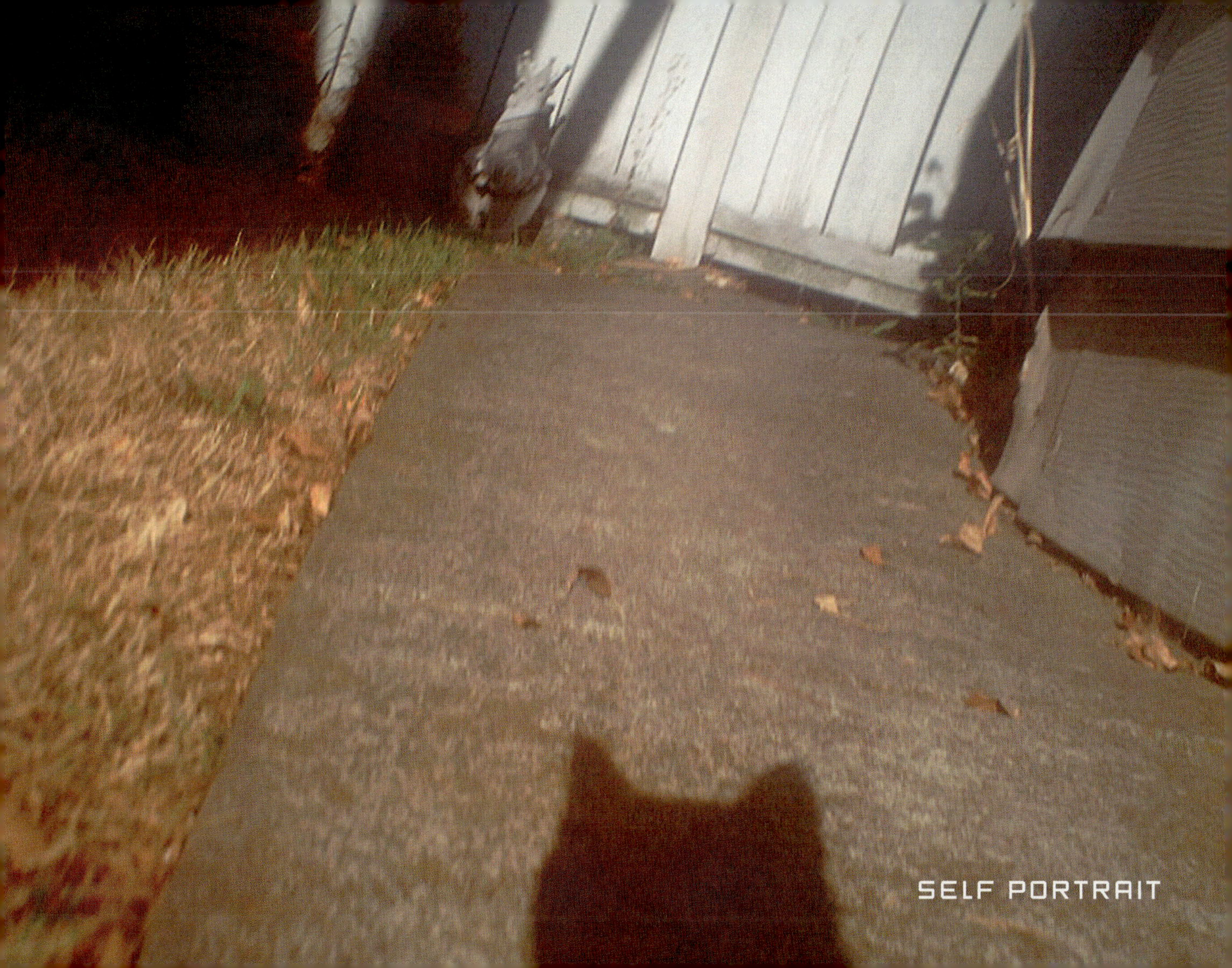
SELF PORTRAIT

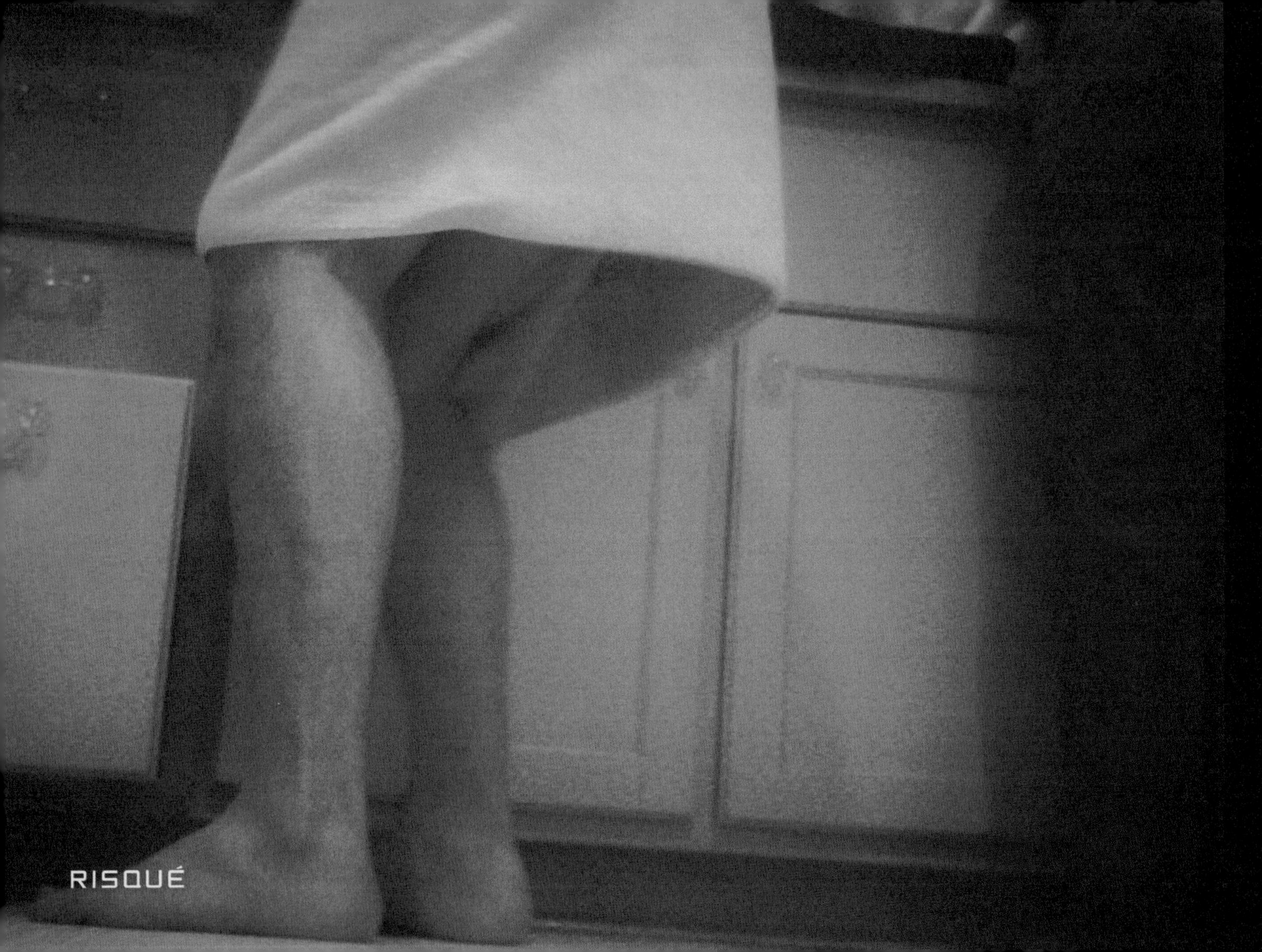
RISQUÉ

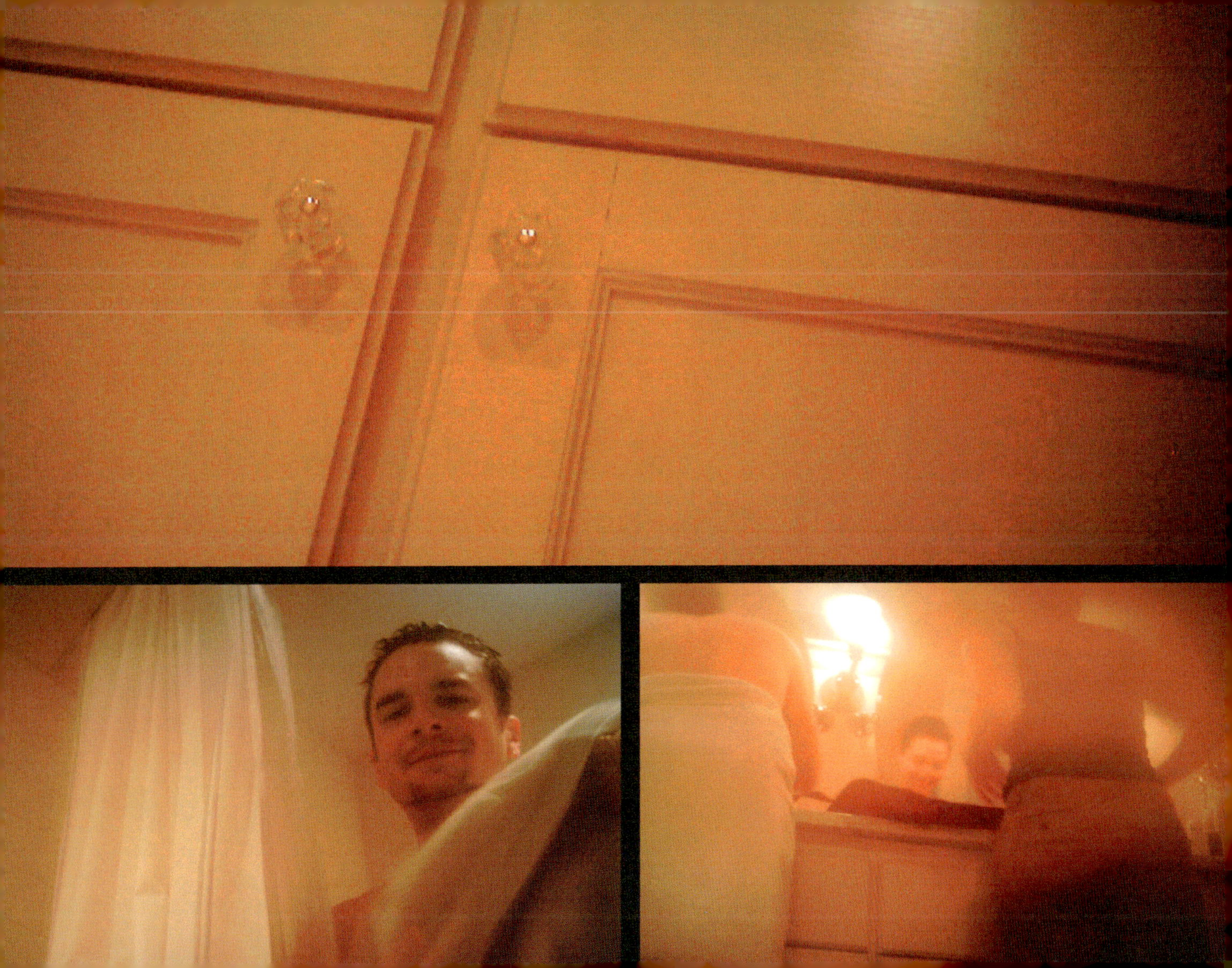

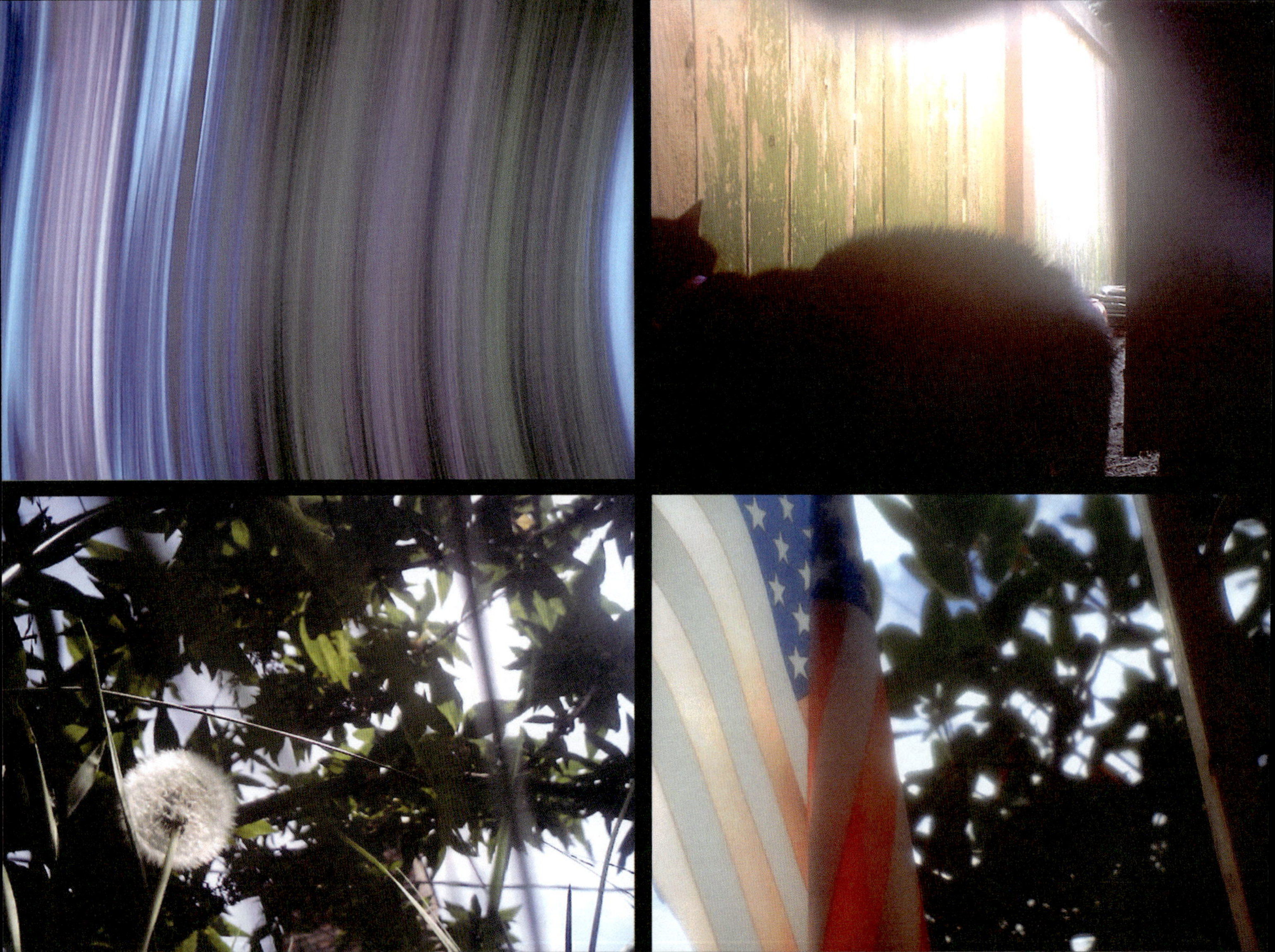

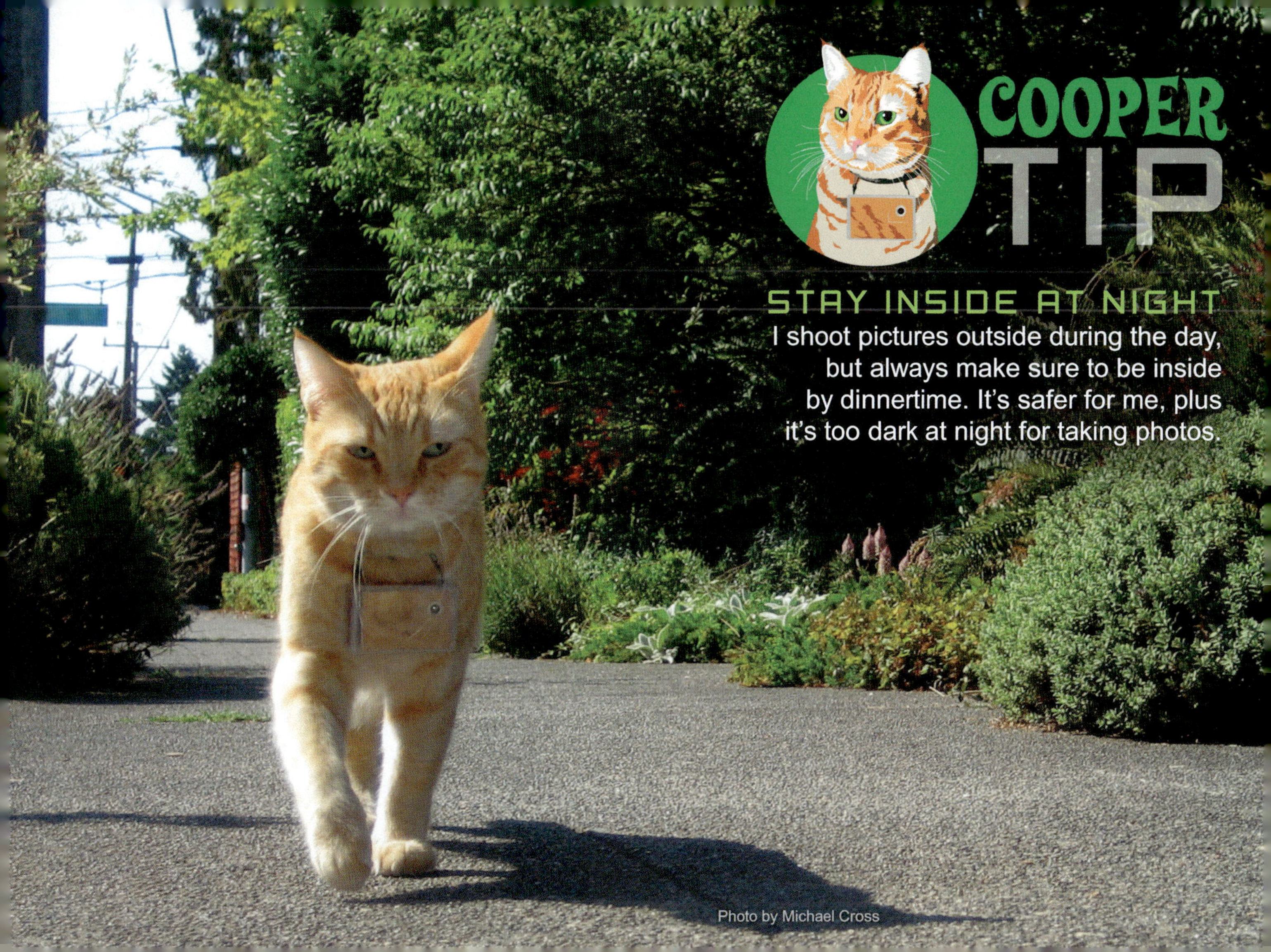


Photo by Michael Cross

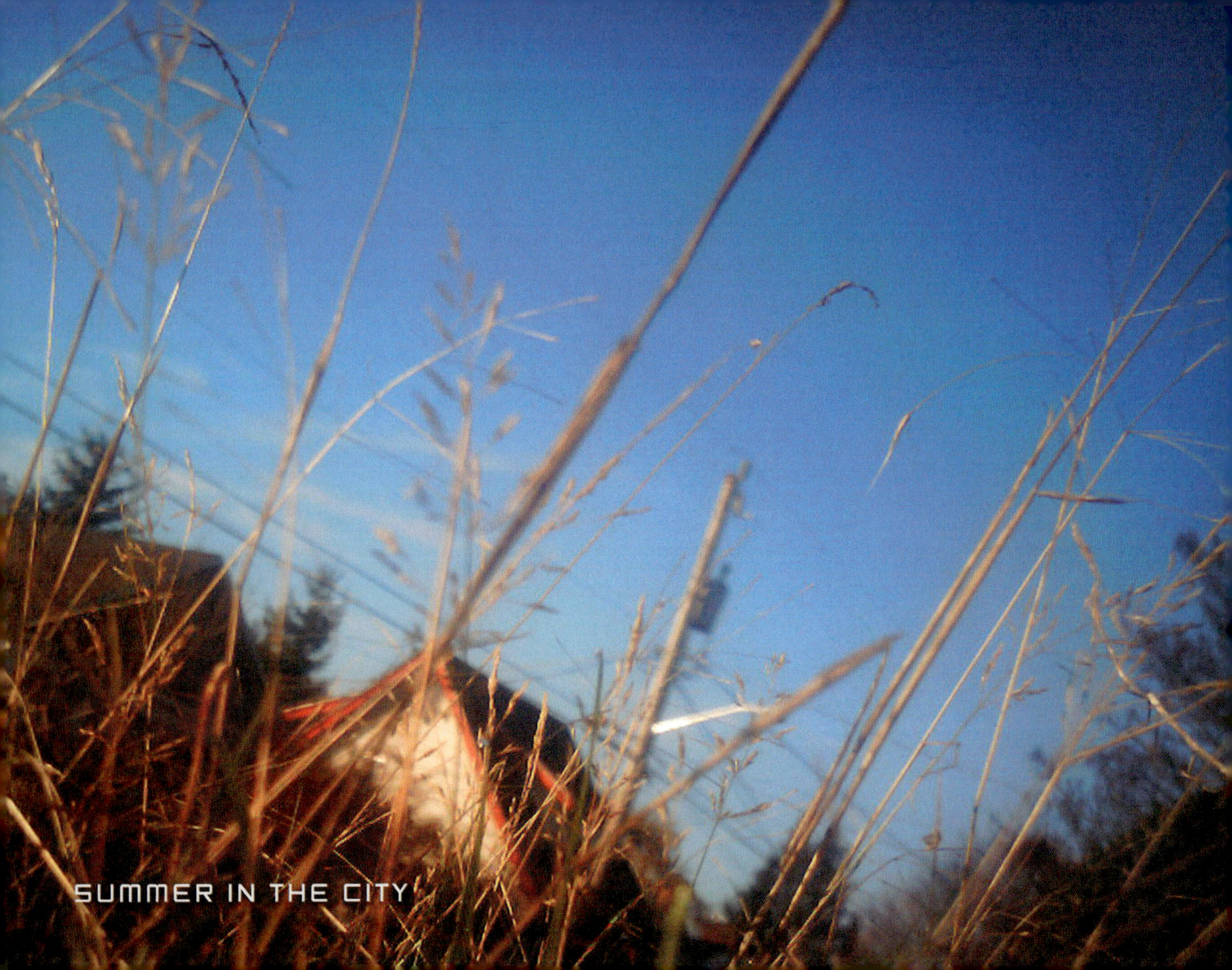
SUMMER IN THE CITY

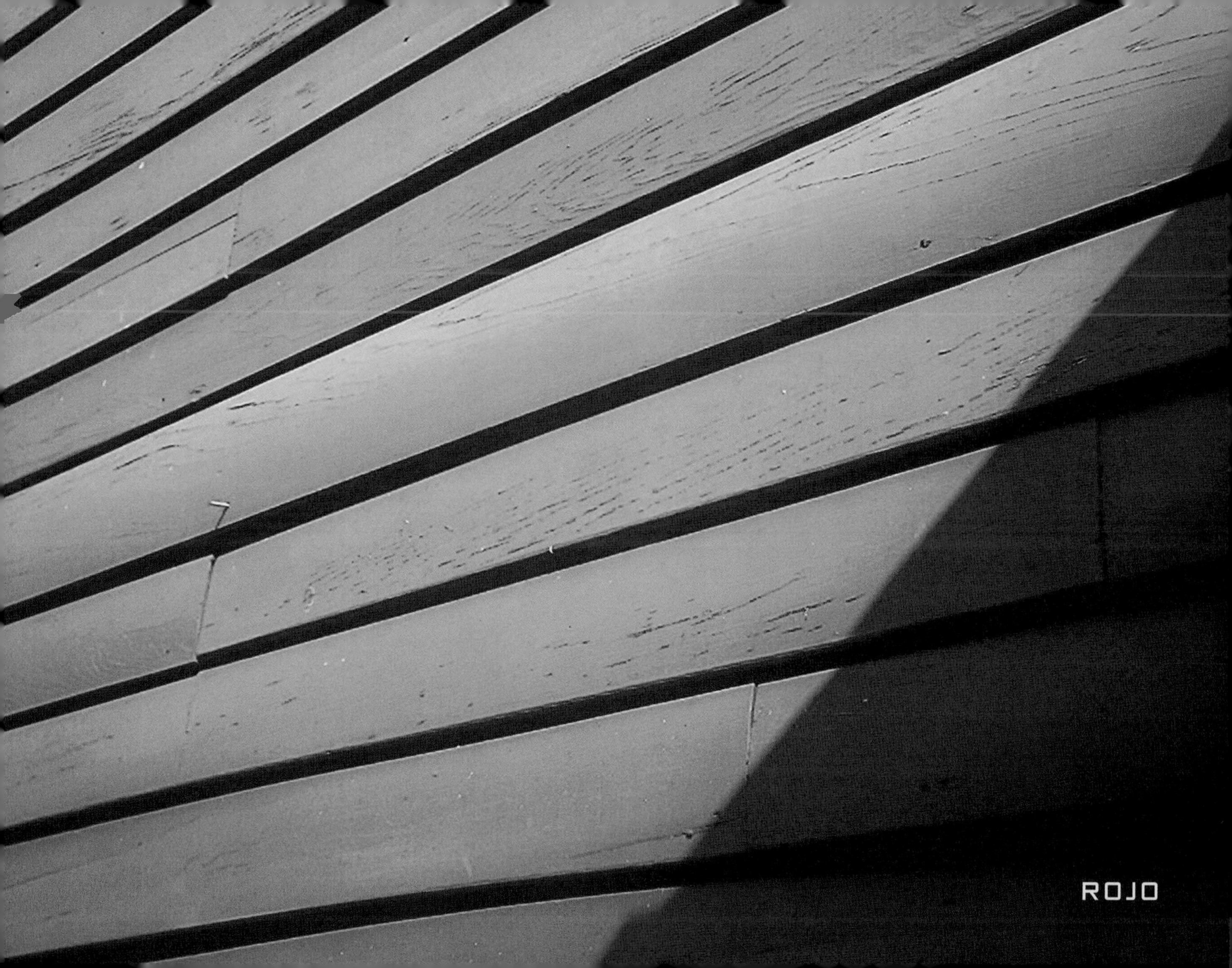
ROJO

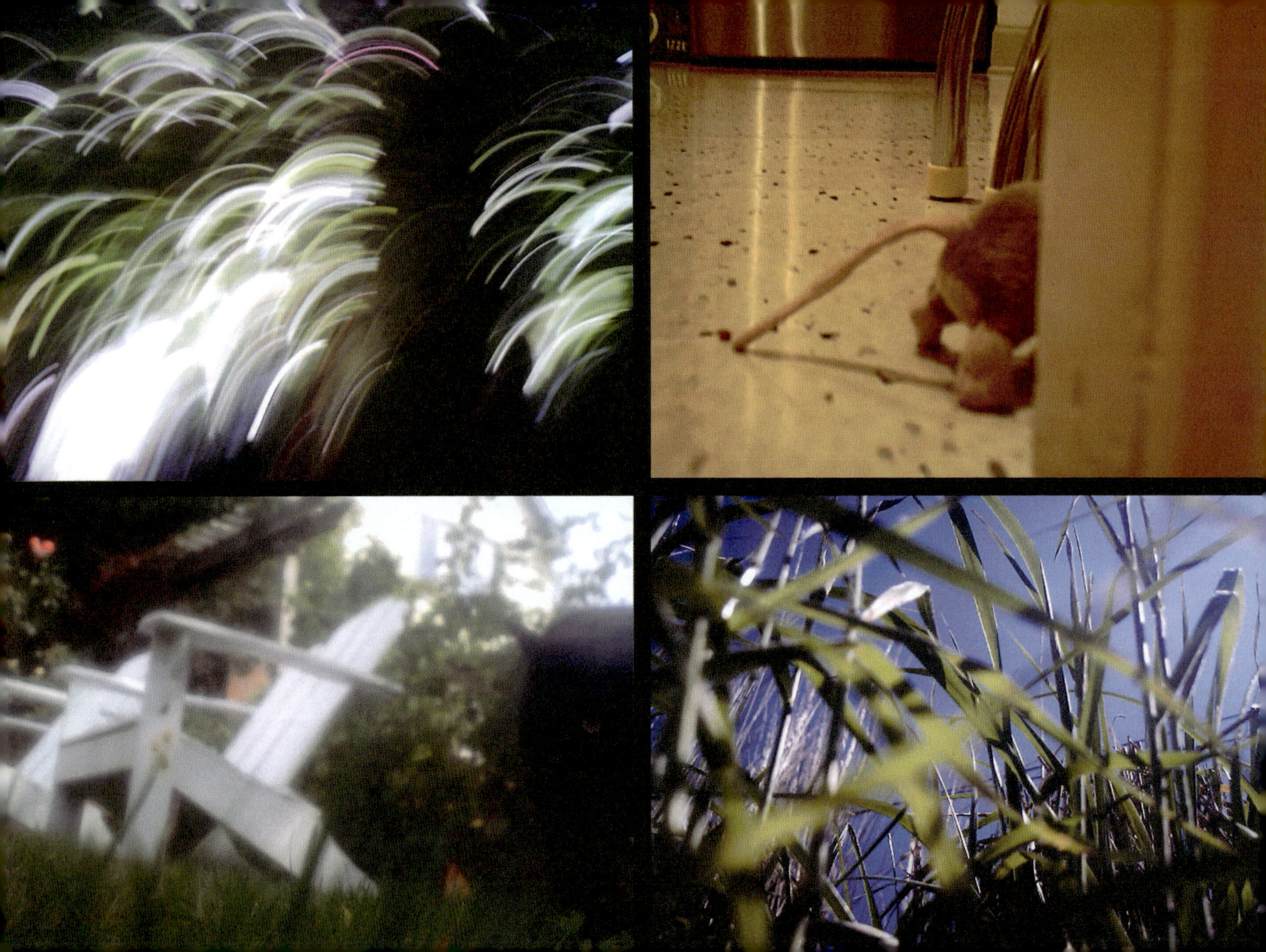

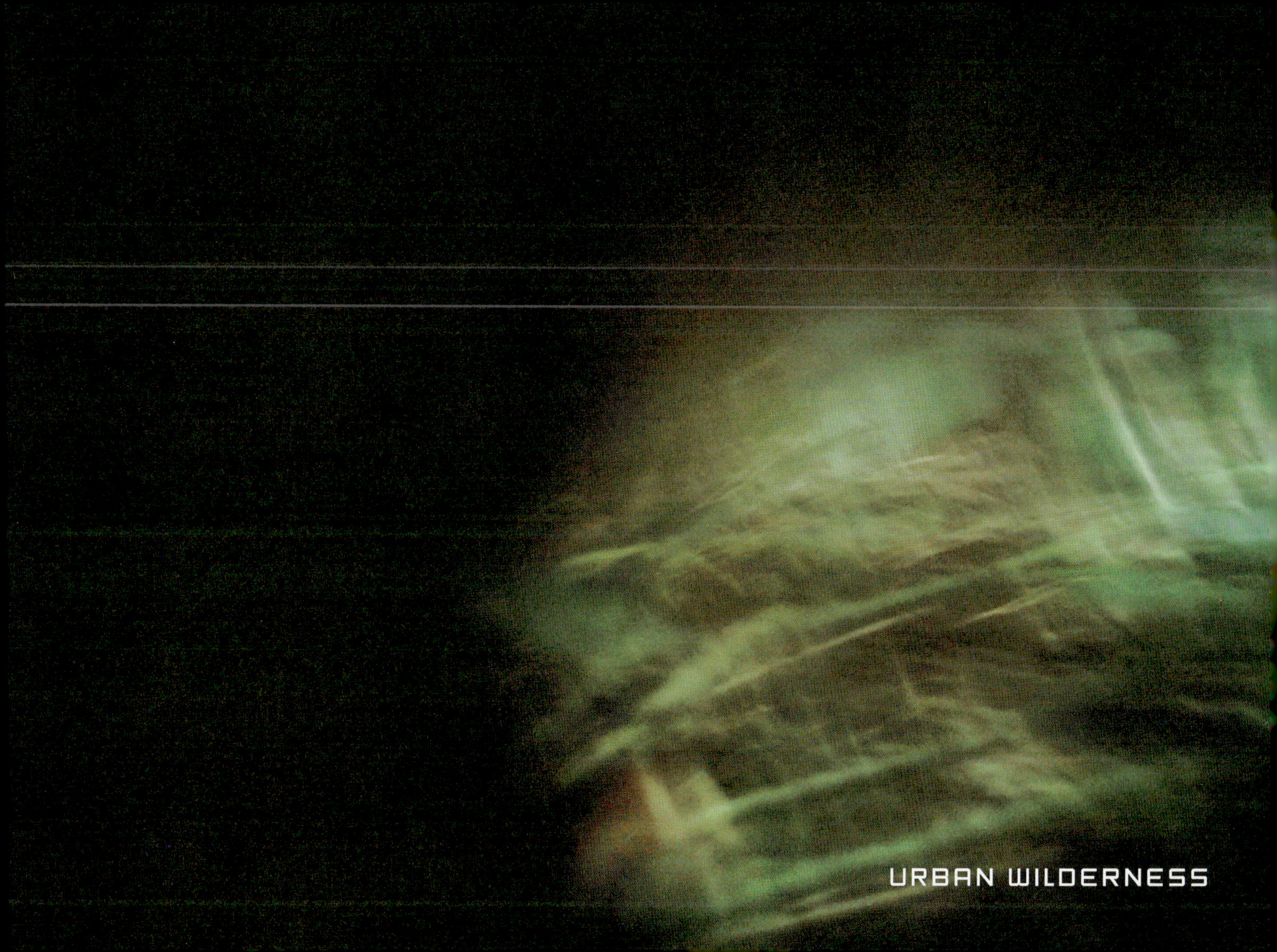
URBAN WILDERNESS

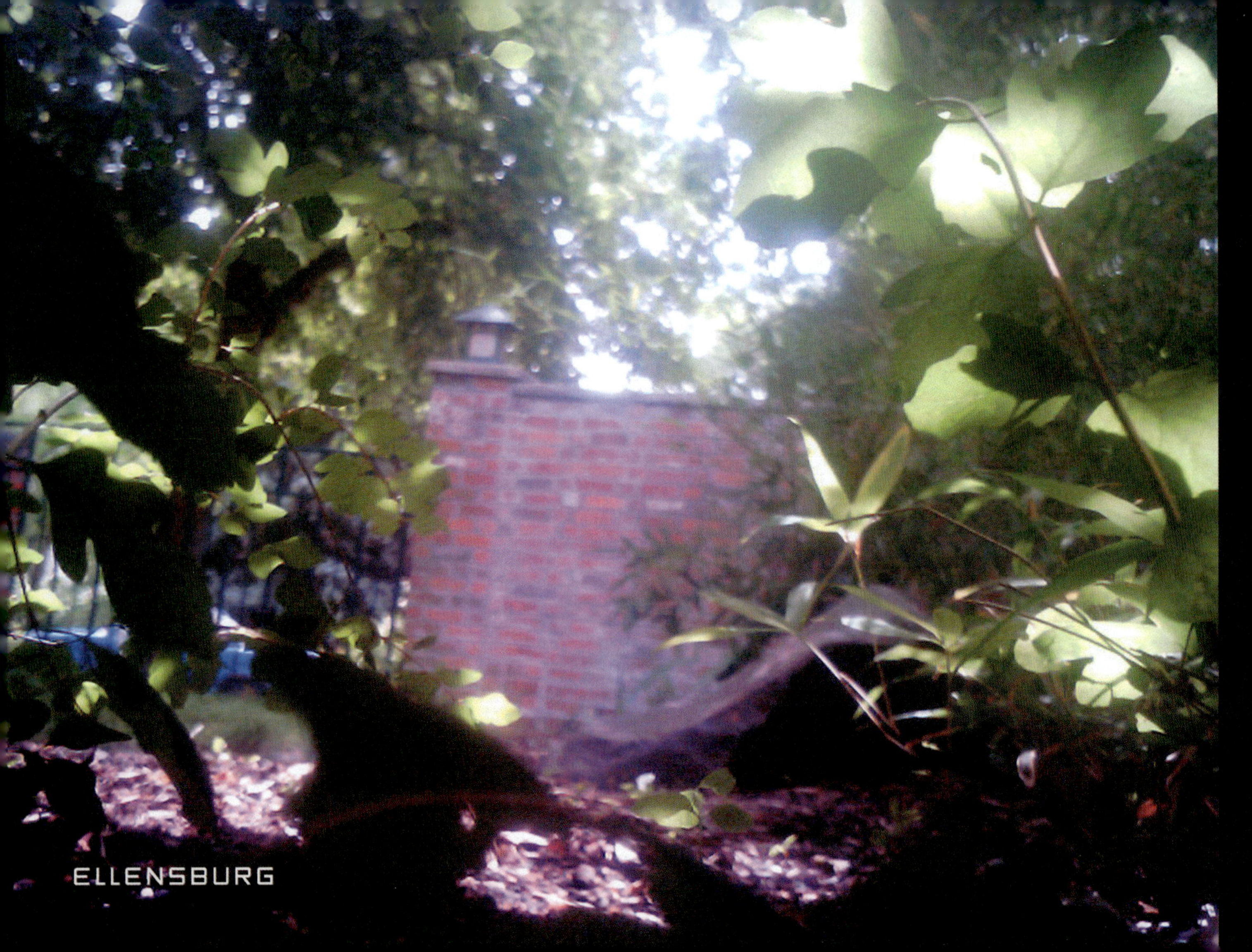

ELLENSBURG

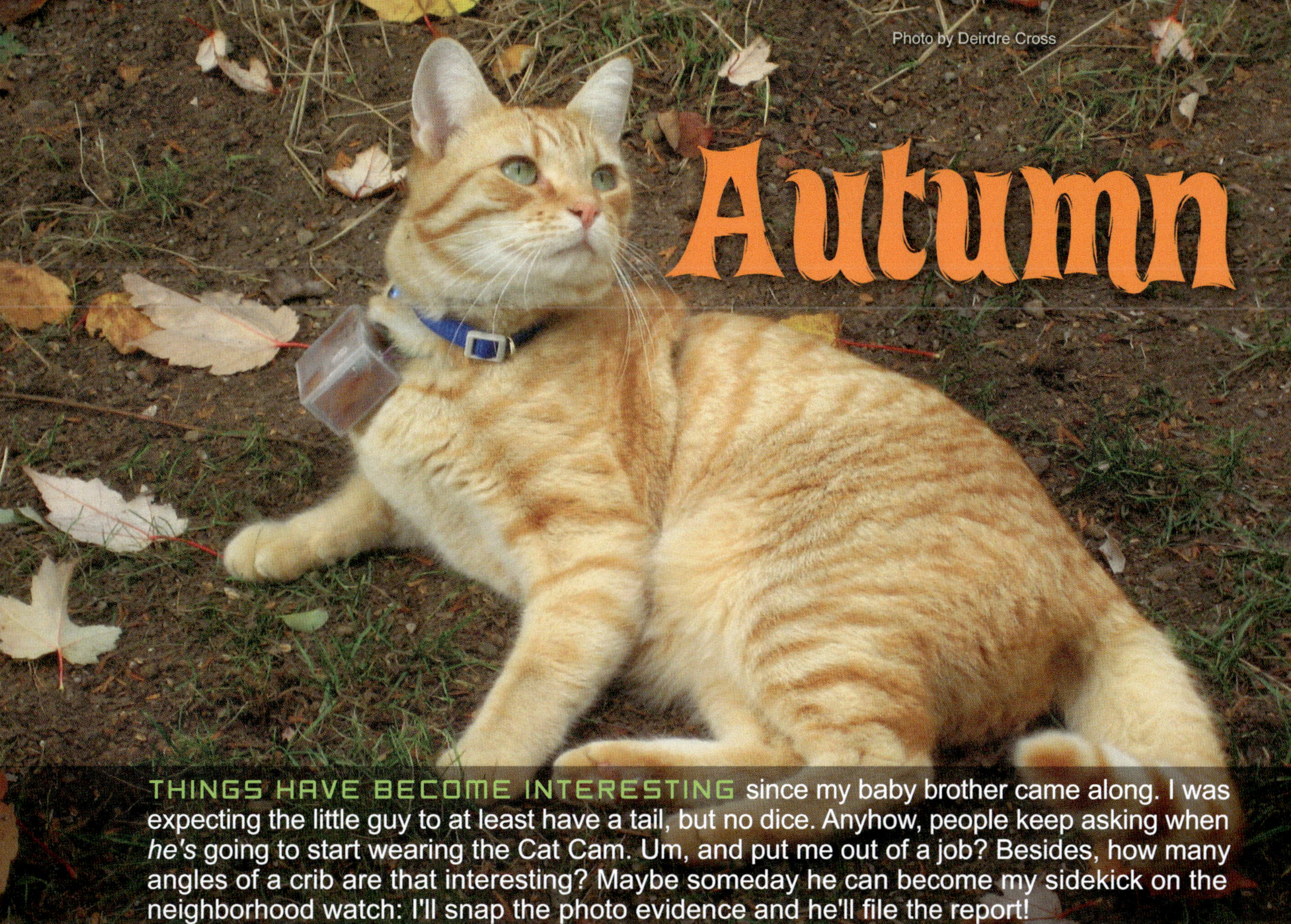
Photo by Deirdre Cross

# Autumn

THINGS HAVE BECOME INTERESTING since my baby brother came along. I was expecting the little guy to at least have a tail, but no dice. Anyhow, people keep asking when *he's* going to start wearing the Cat Cam. Um, and put me out of a job? Besides, how many angles of a crib are that interesting? Maybe someday he can become my sidekick on the neighborhood watch: I'll snap the photo evidence and he'll file the report!

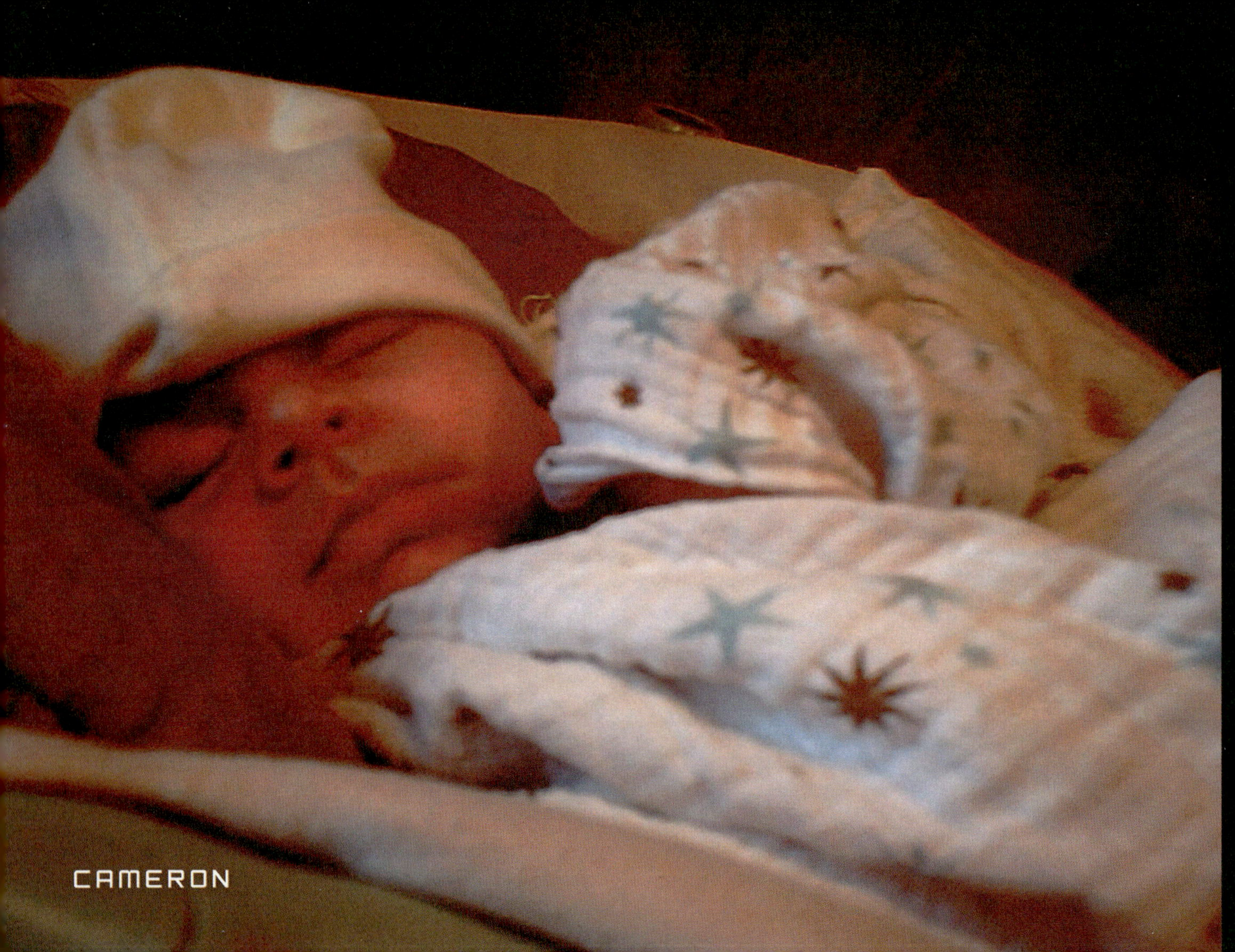
CAMERON

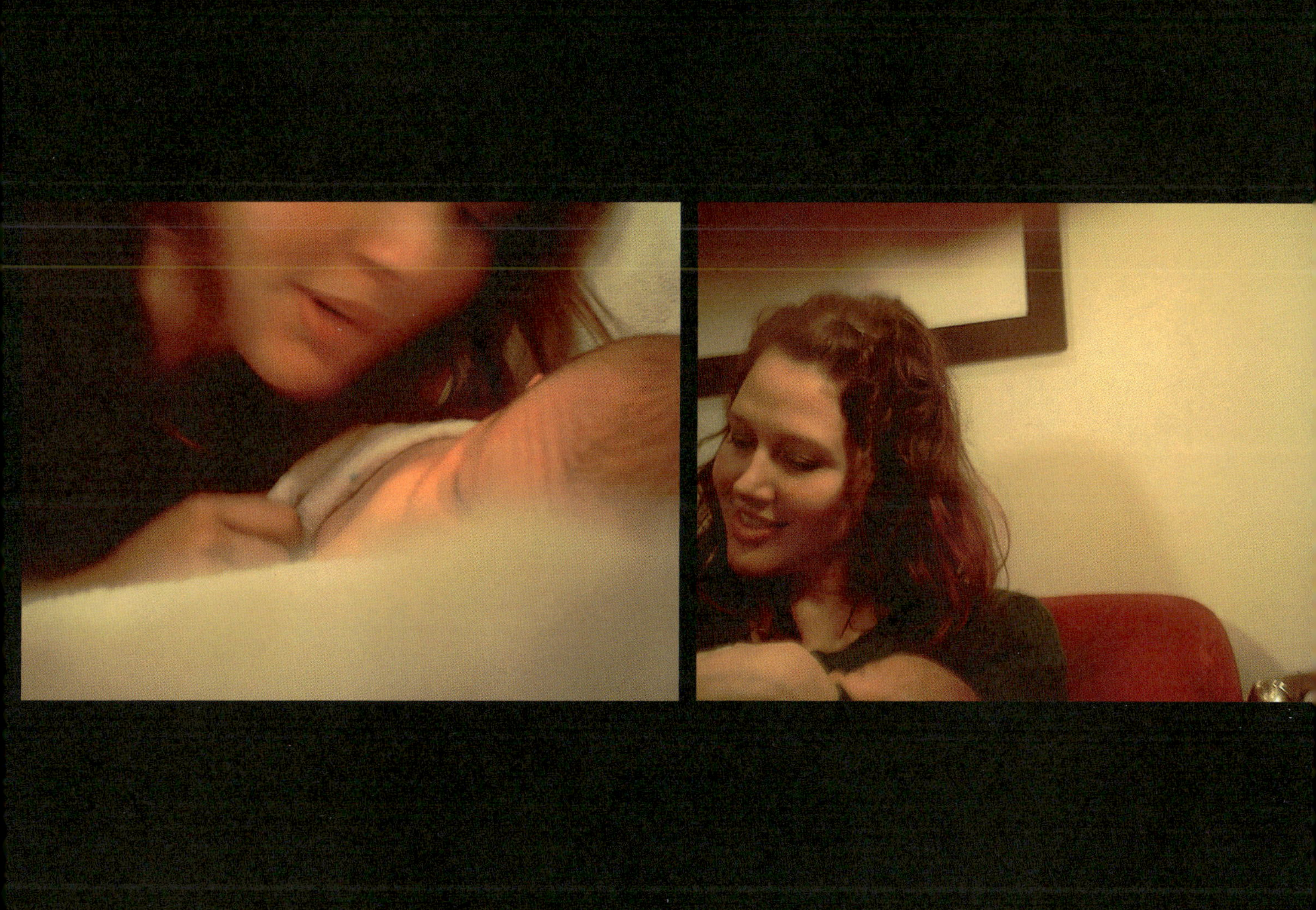

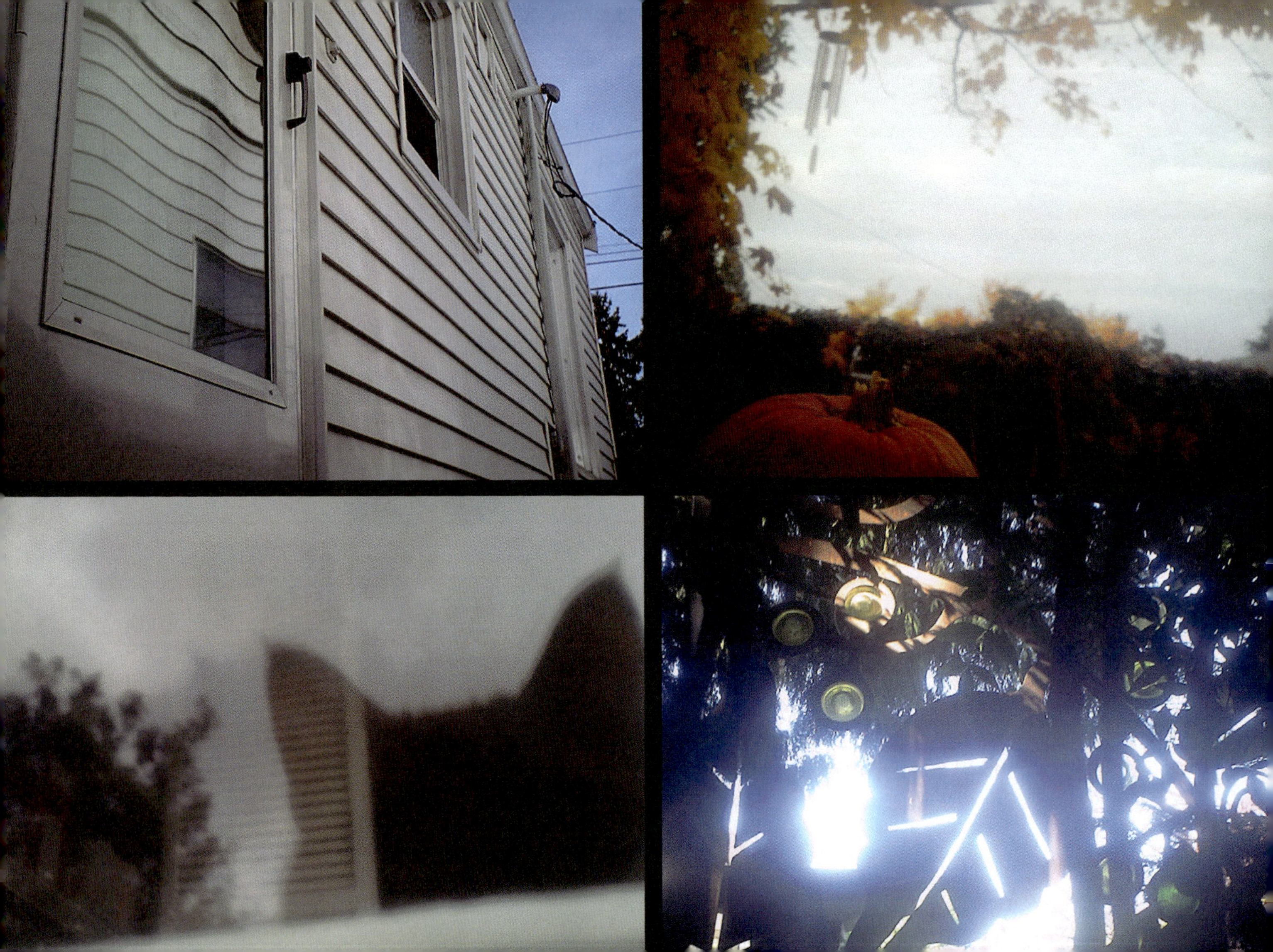

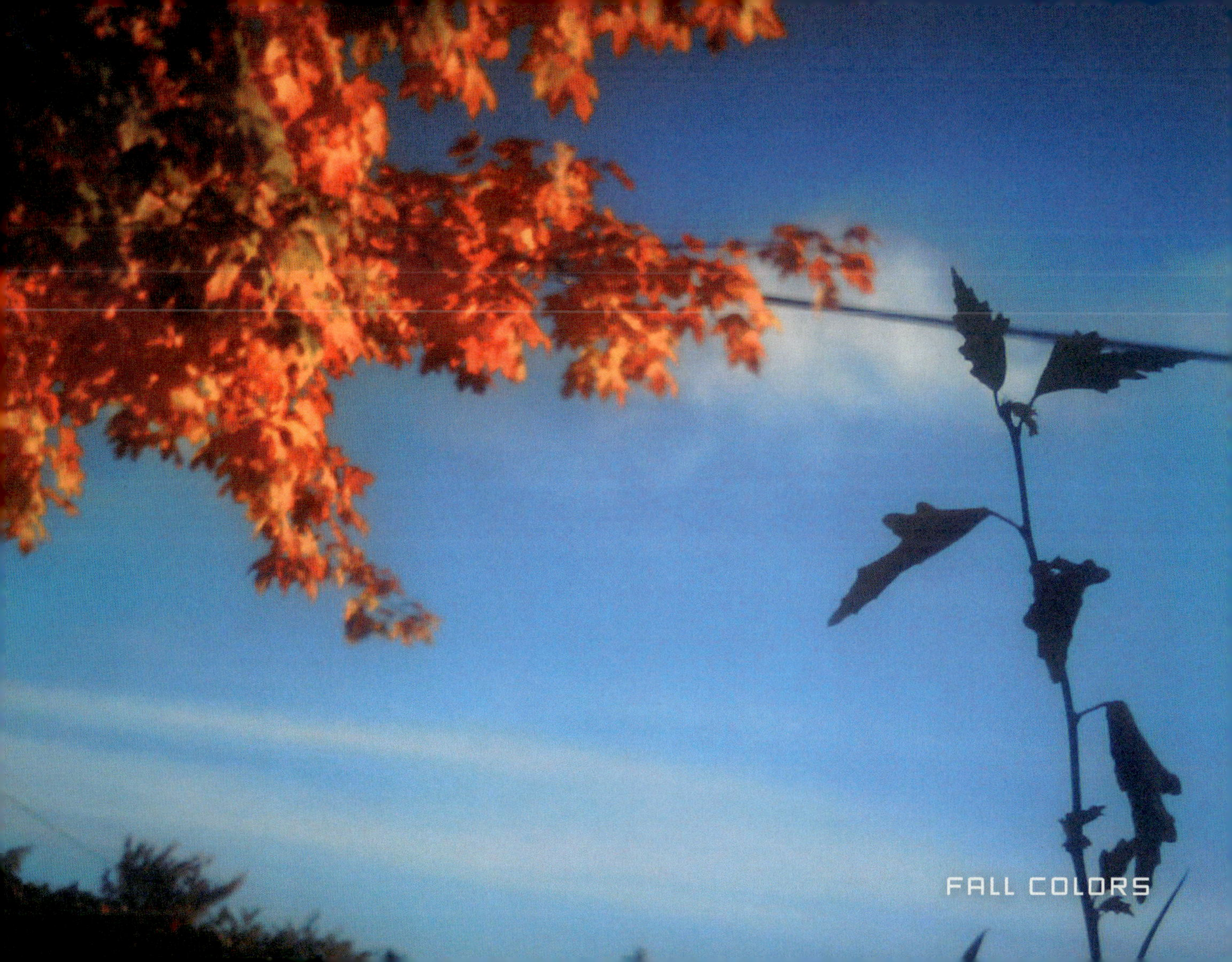
FALL COLORS

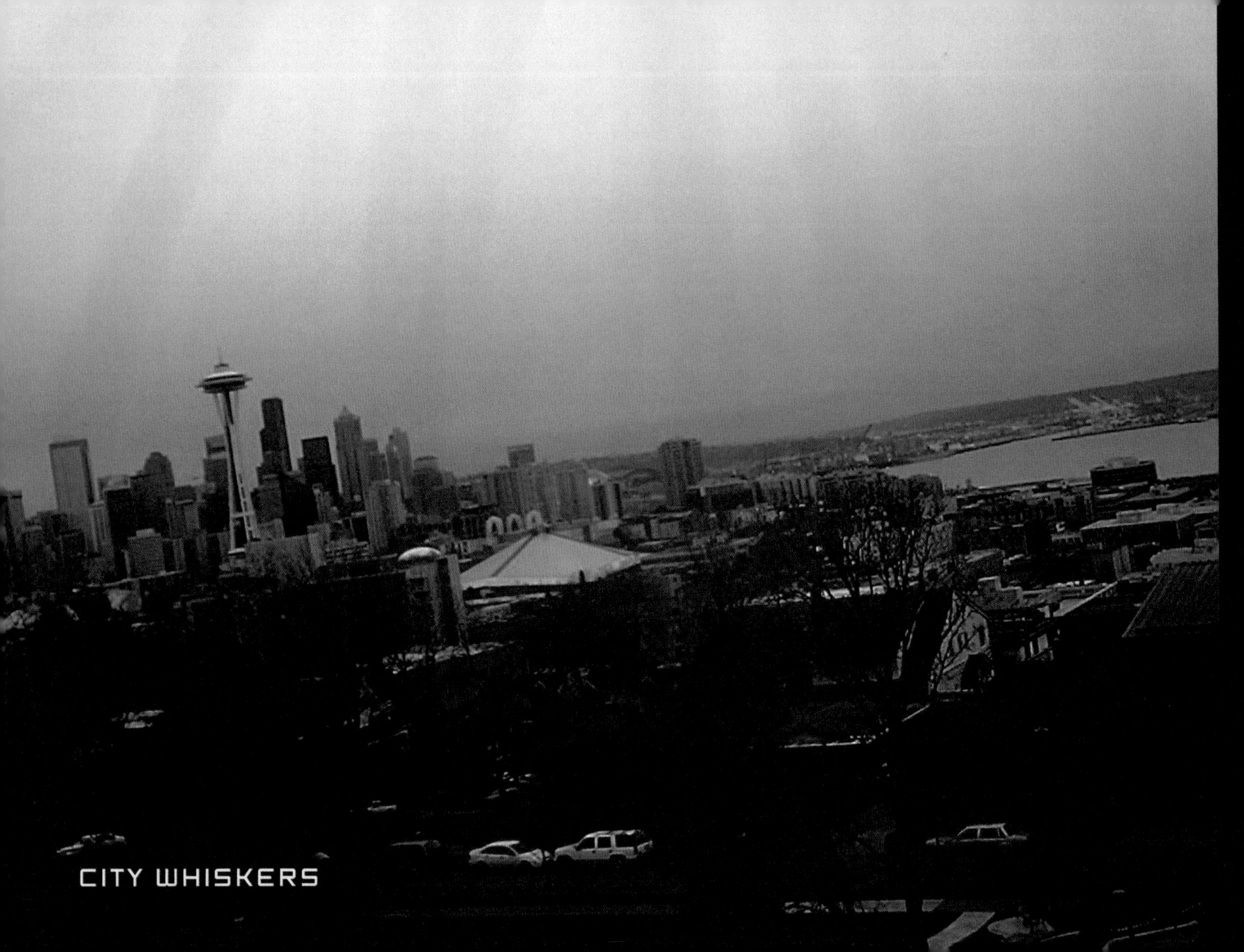
CITY WHISKERS

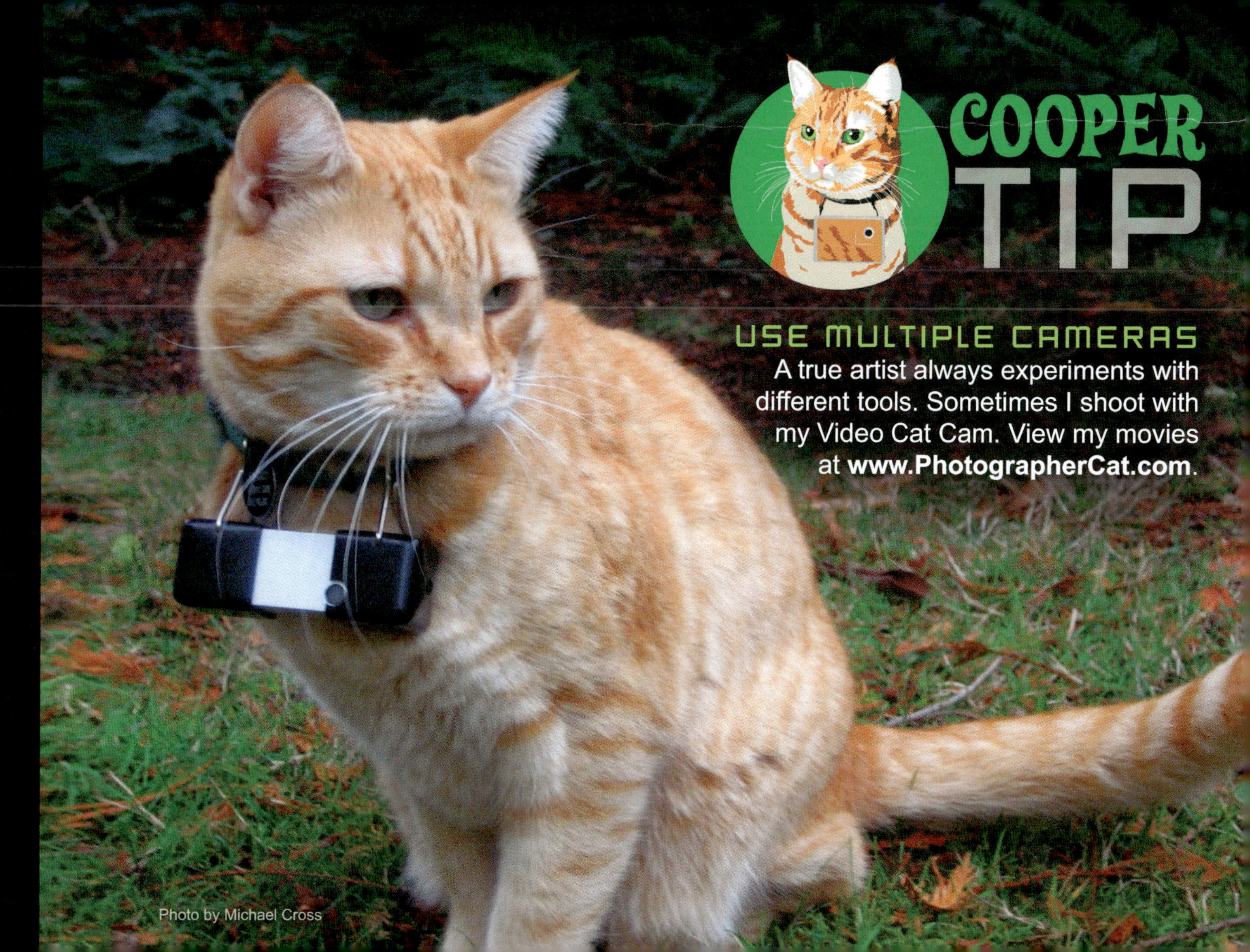
COOPER
TIP
USE MULTIPLE CAMERAS
A true artist always experiments with different tools. Sometimes I shoot with my Video Cat Cam. View my movies at **www.PhotographerCat.com**.
Photo by Michael Cross

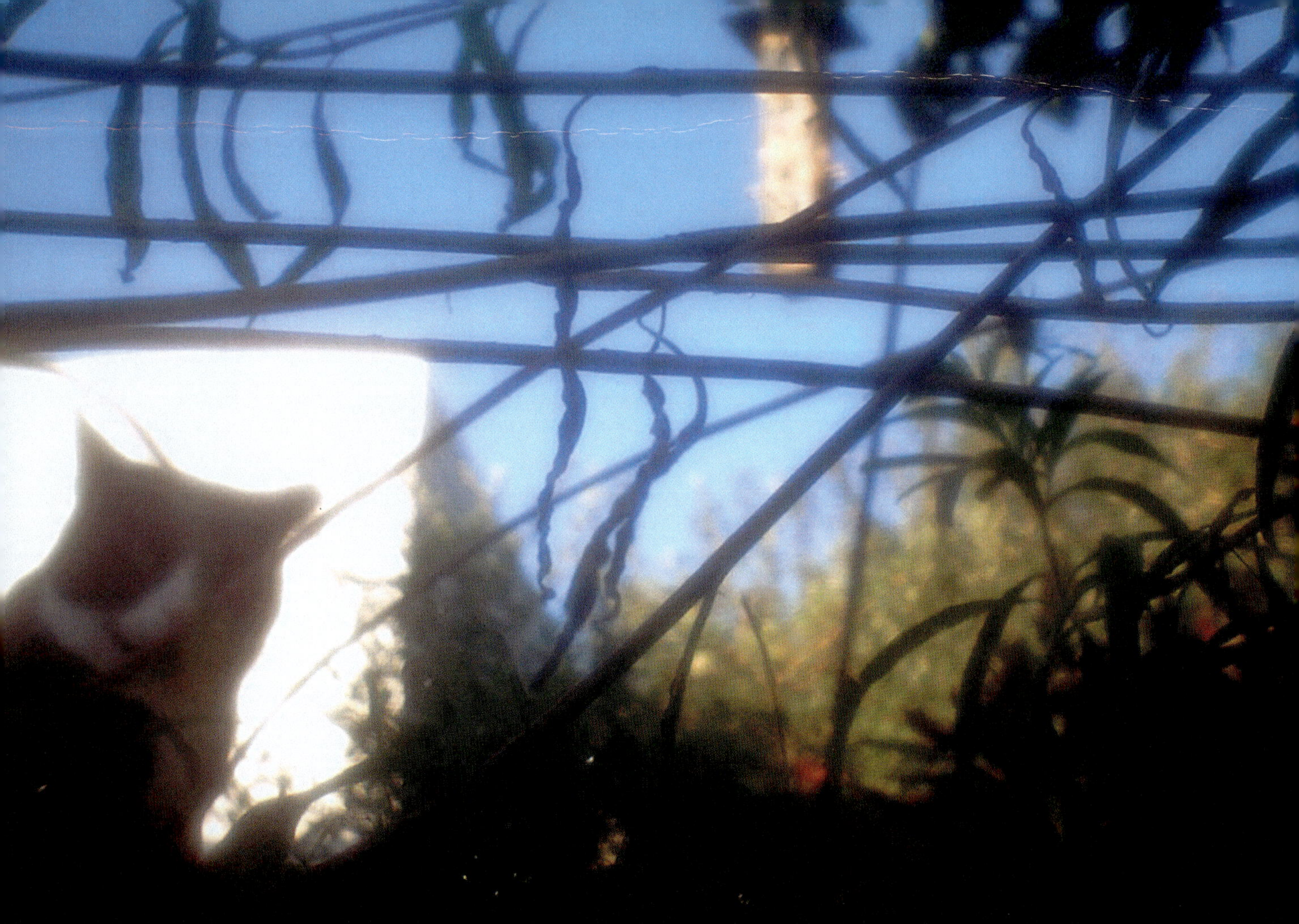

BIRD FEEDER

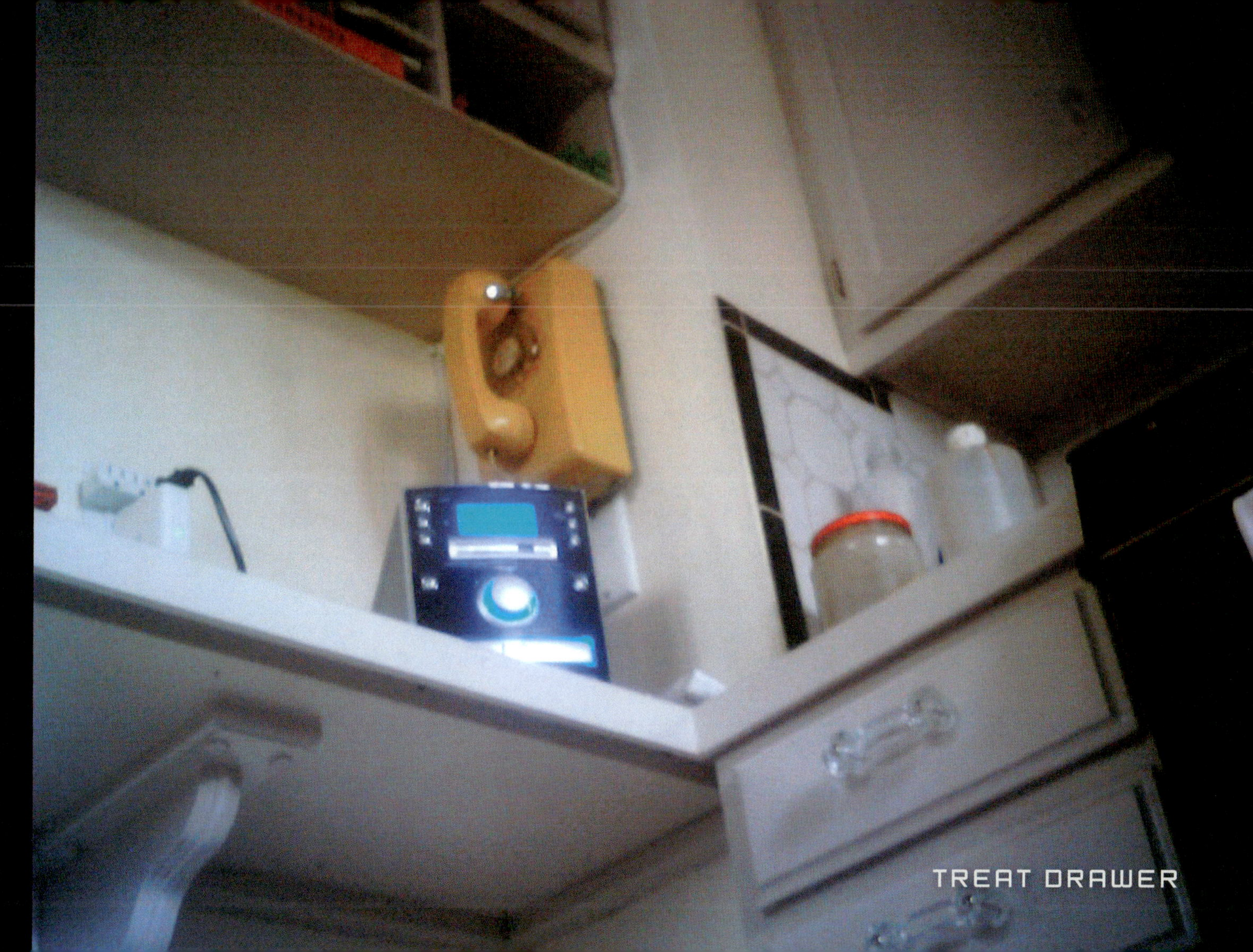
TREAT DRAWER

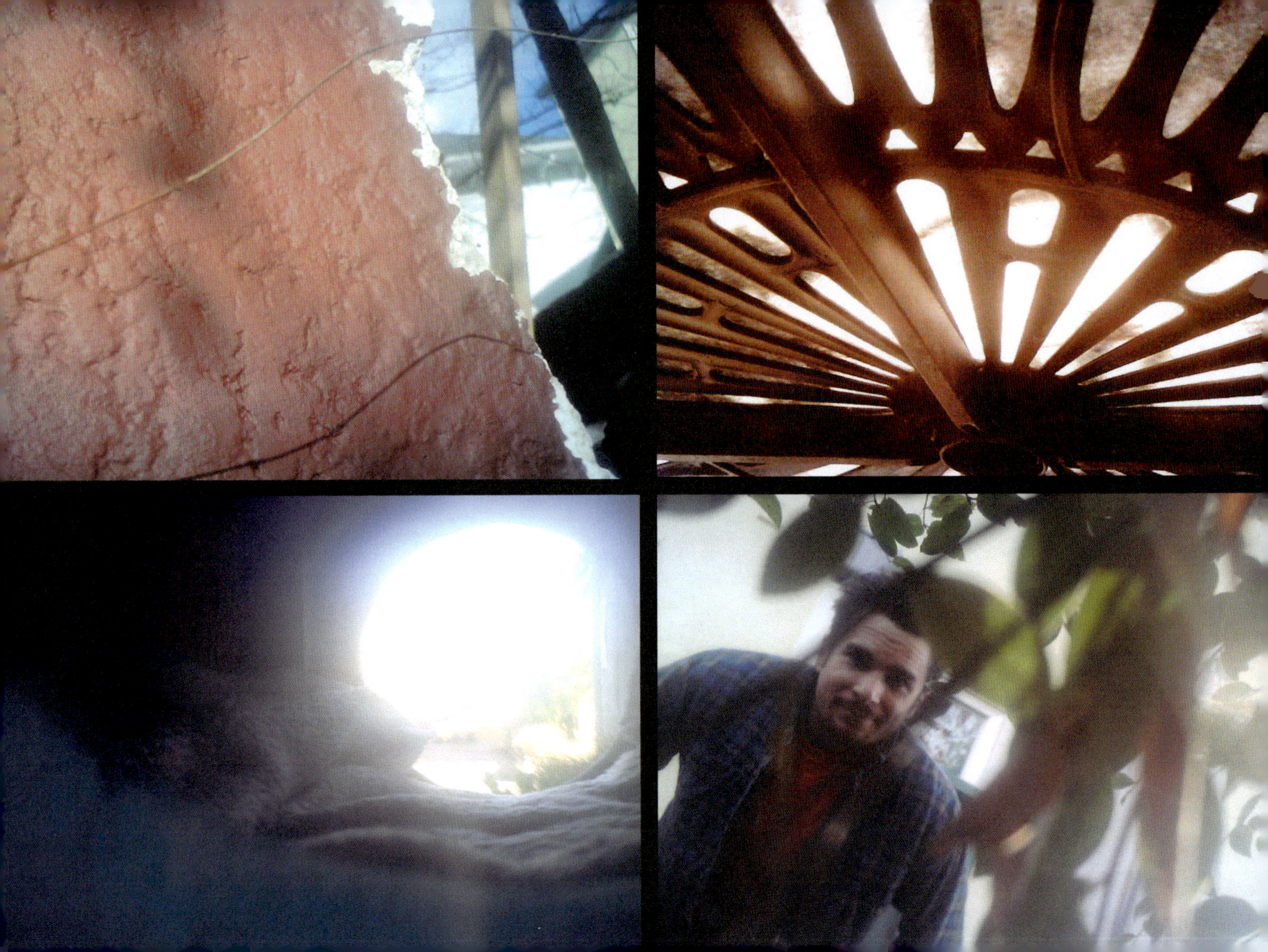

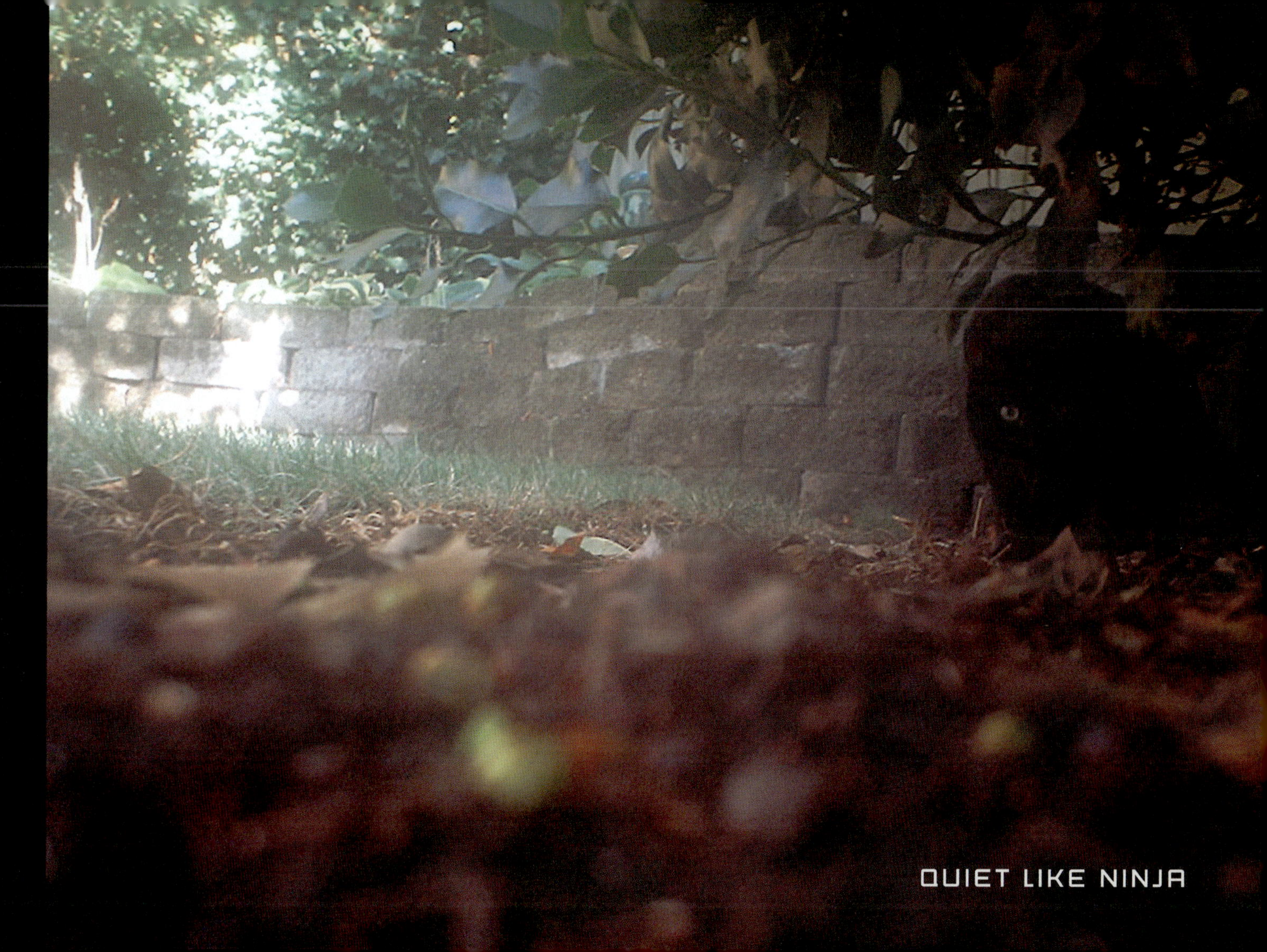

QUIET LIKE NINJA

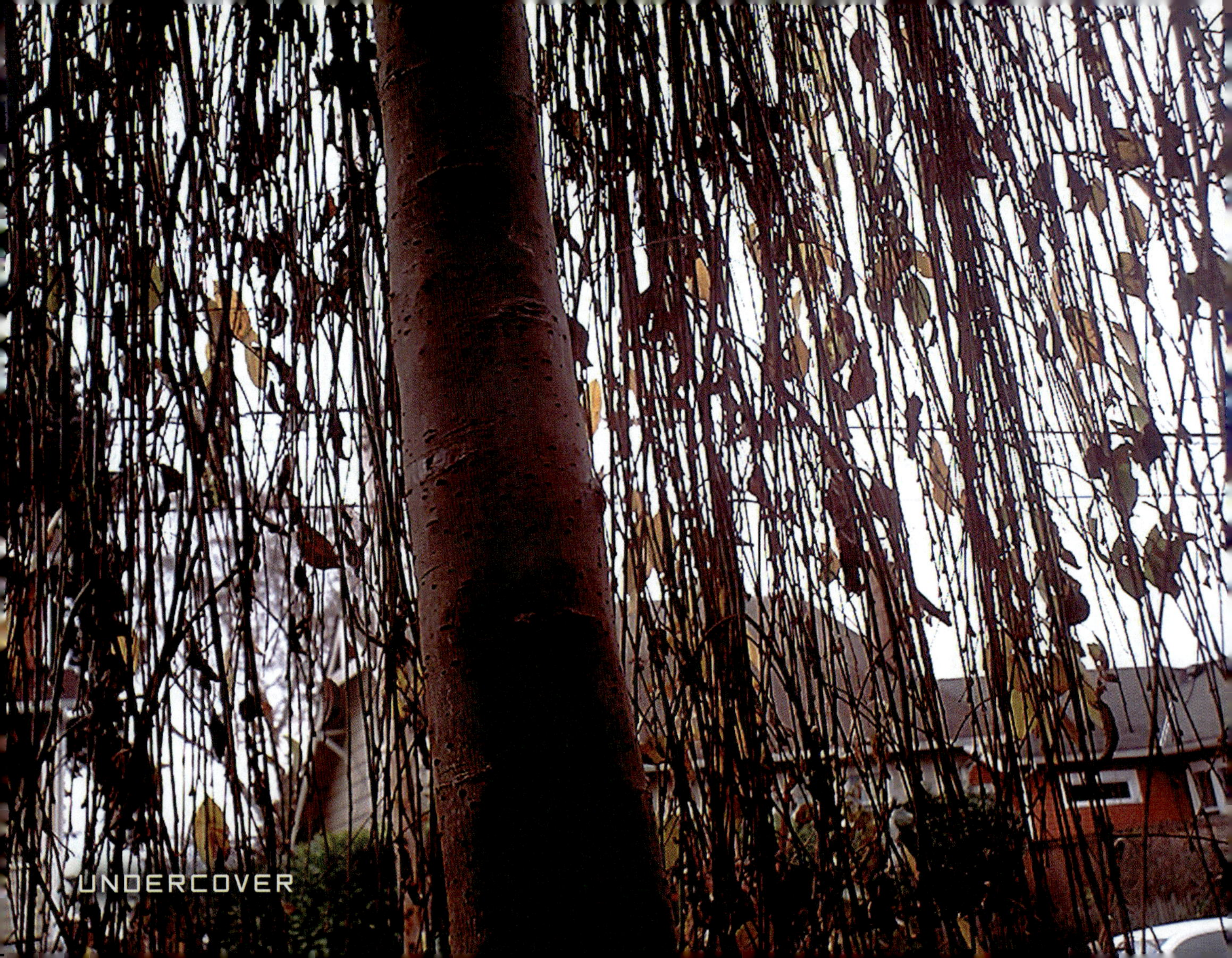
UNDERCOVER

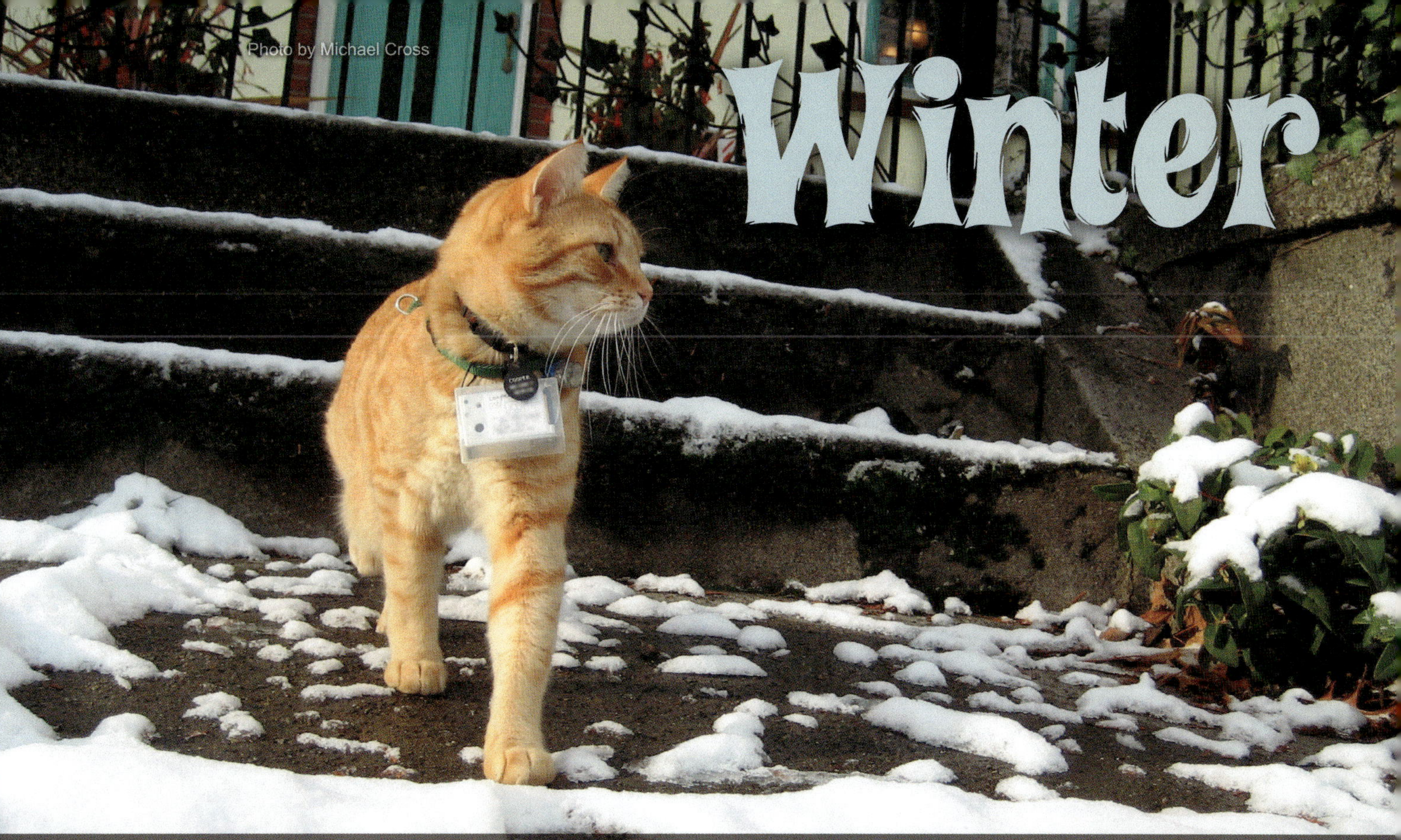


# Winter

THERE ARE TWO DRAWBACKS of wintertime. One: Frozen birdbaths. This means empty birdbaths, and that means boredom for old Coopster. Number two: Have you ever had to chew ice from your paws? It's chilling, let me tell you. But it's worth it just to snap a pretty photo of your neighborhood in the snow. And it makes going inside for shrimp snacks all the tastier, right? Number one *benefit* of wintertime: Humans are much more likely to let me snuggle with them at night.

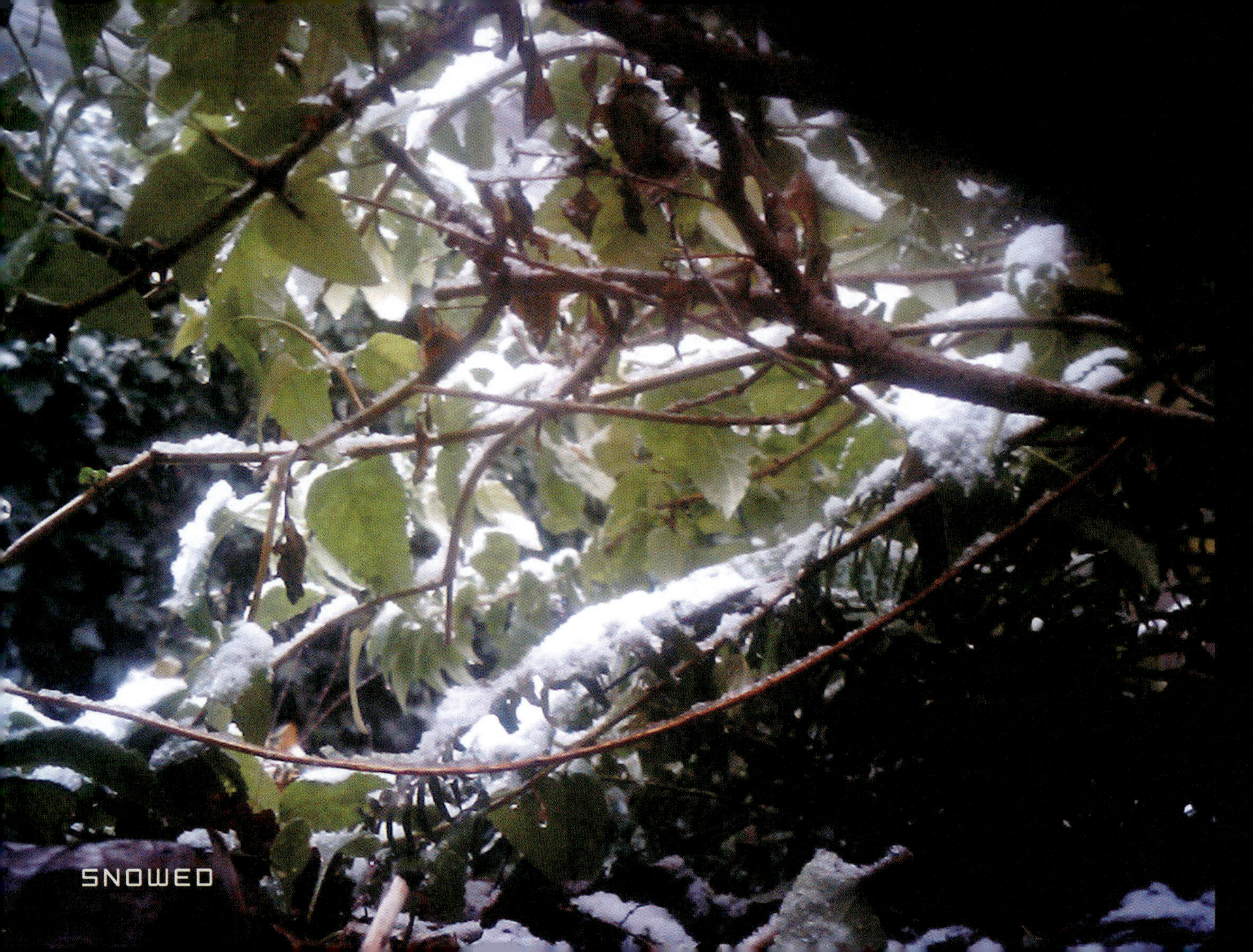

SNOWED

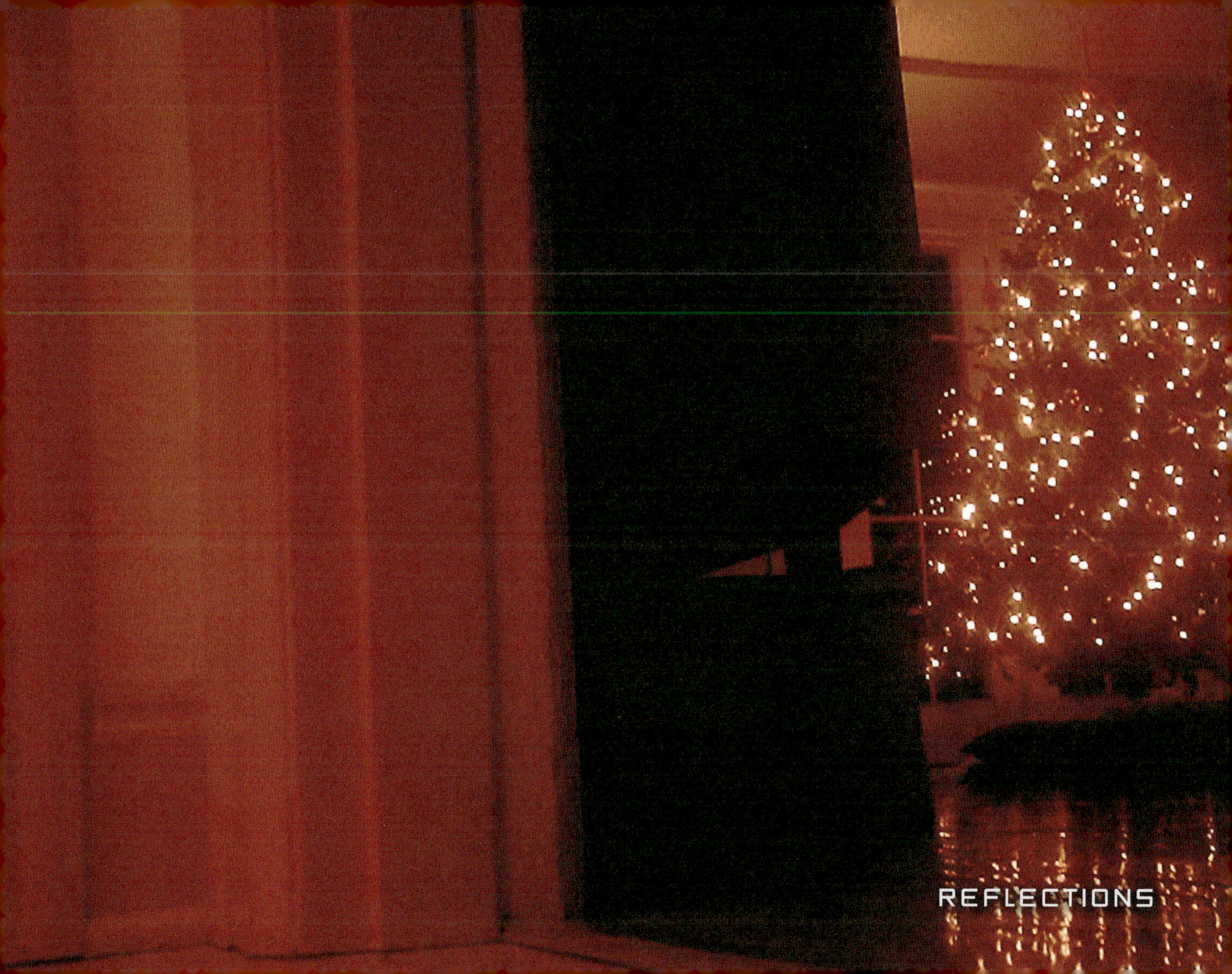
REFLECTIONS

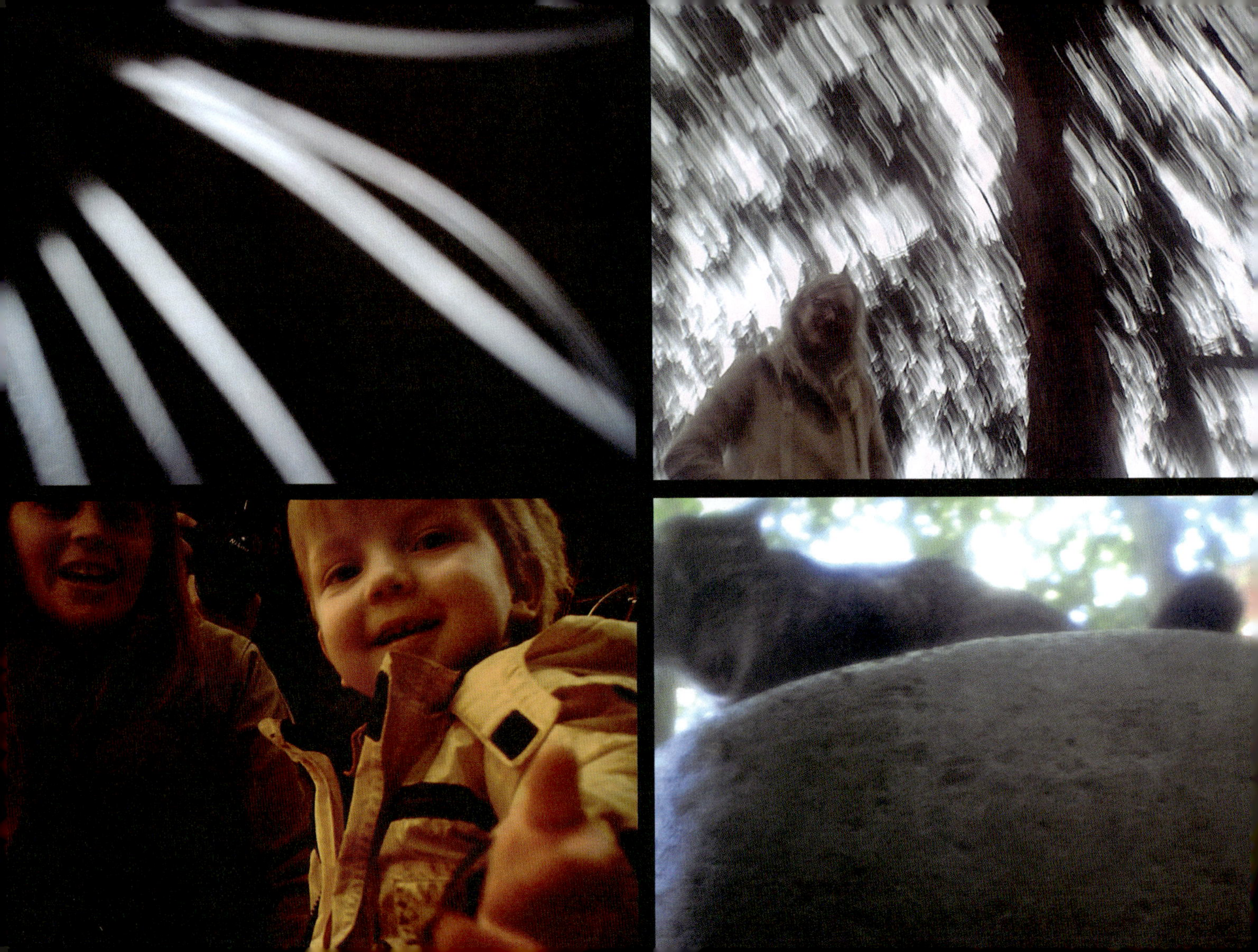

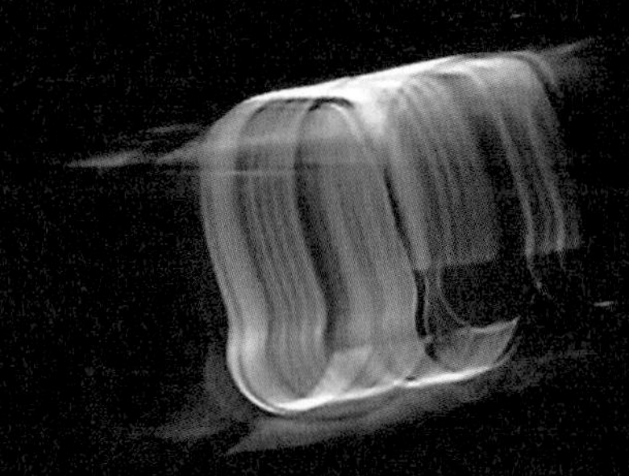

PHANTOM

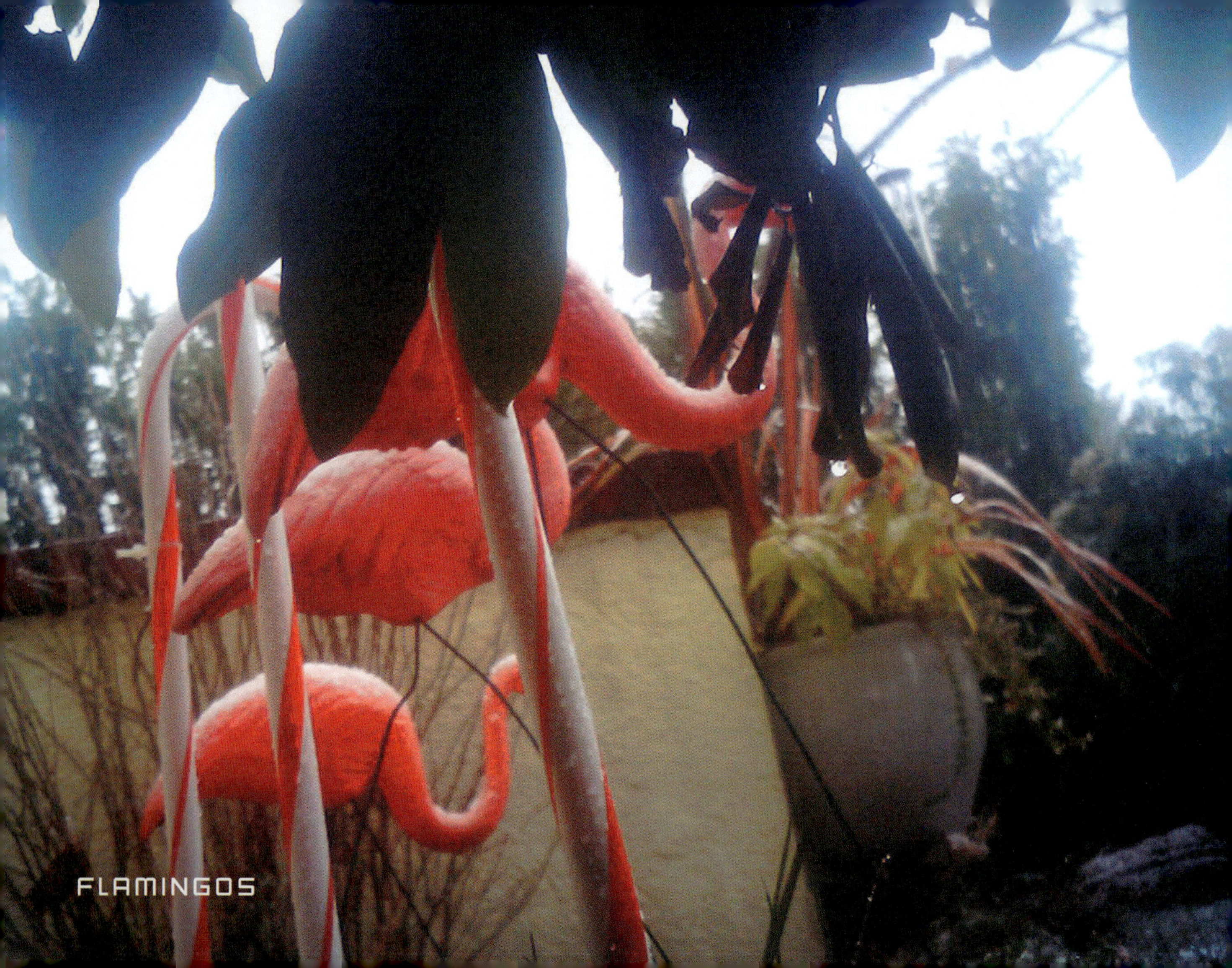

FLAMINGOS

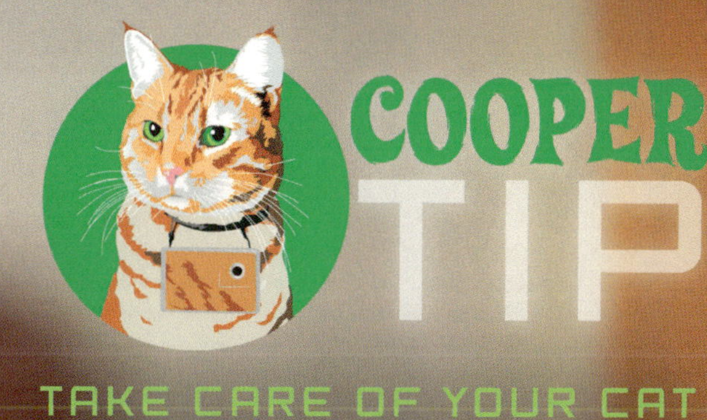


## TAKE CARE OF YOUR CAT

It is very important, for many reasons, to spay and neuter your cats. Also be sure to keep our vaccinations up to date and our claws trimmed short. A healthy cat is a happy cat!

Photo by One Thousand Words Photography

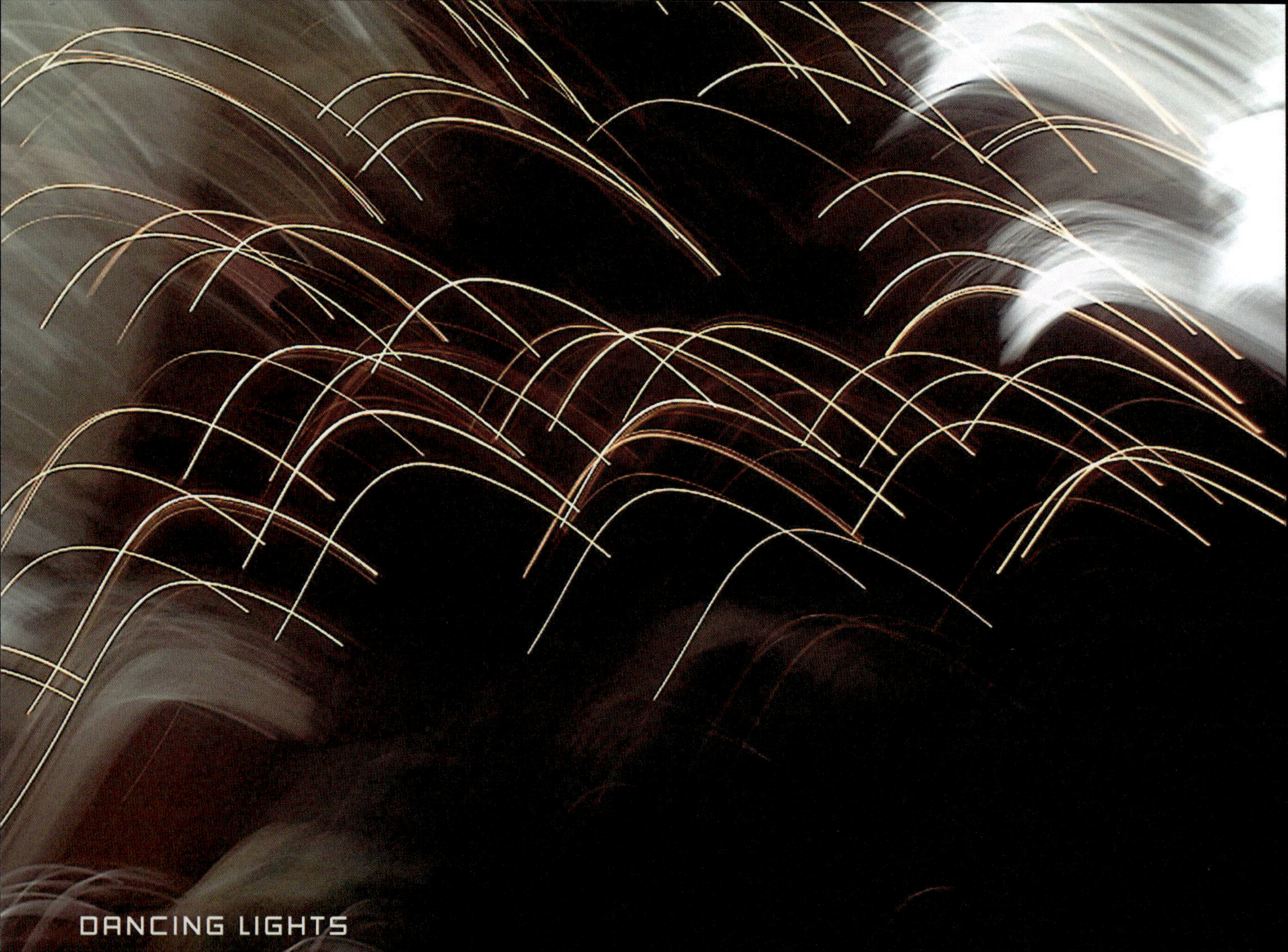

DANCING LIGHTS

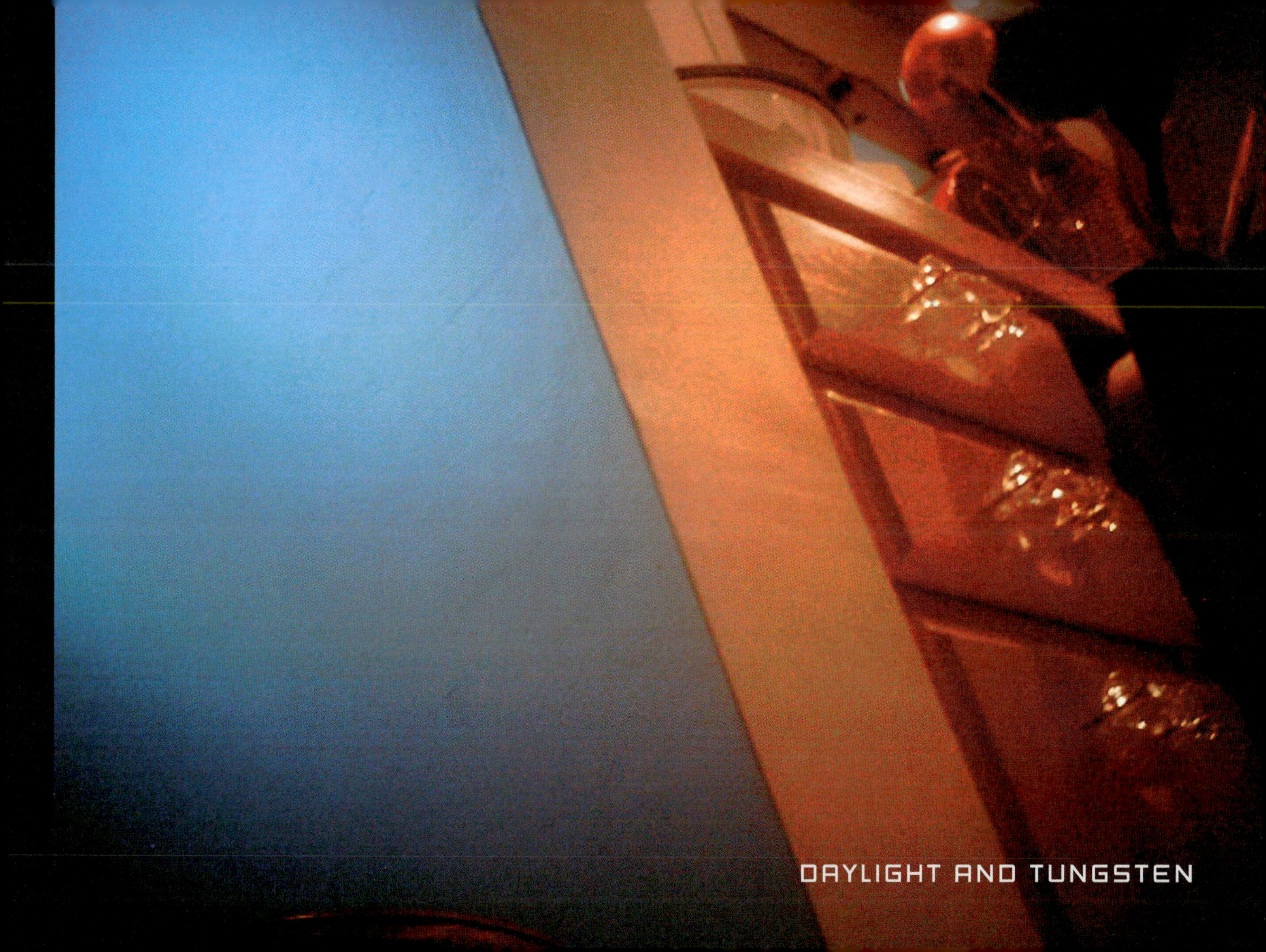
DAYLIGHT AND TUNGSTEN

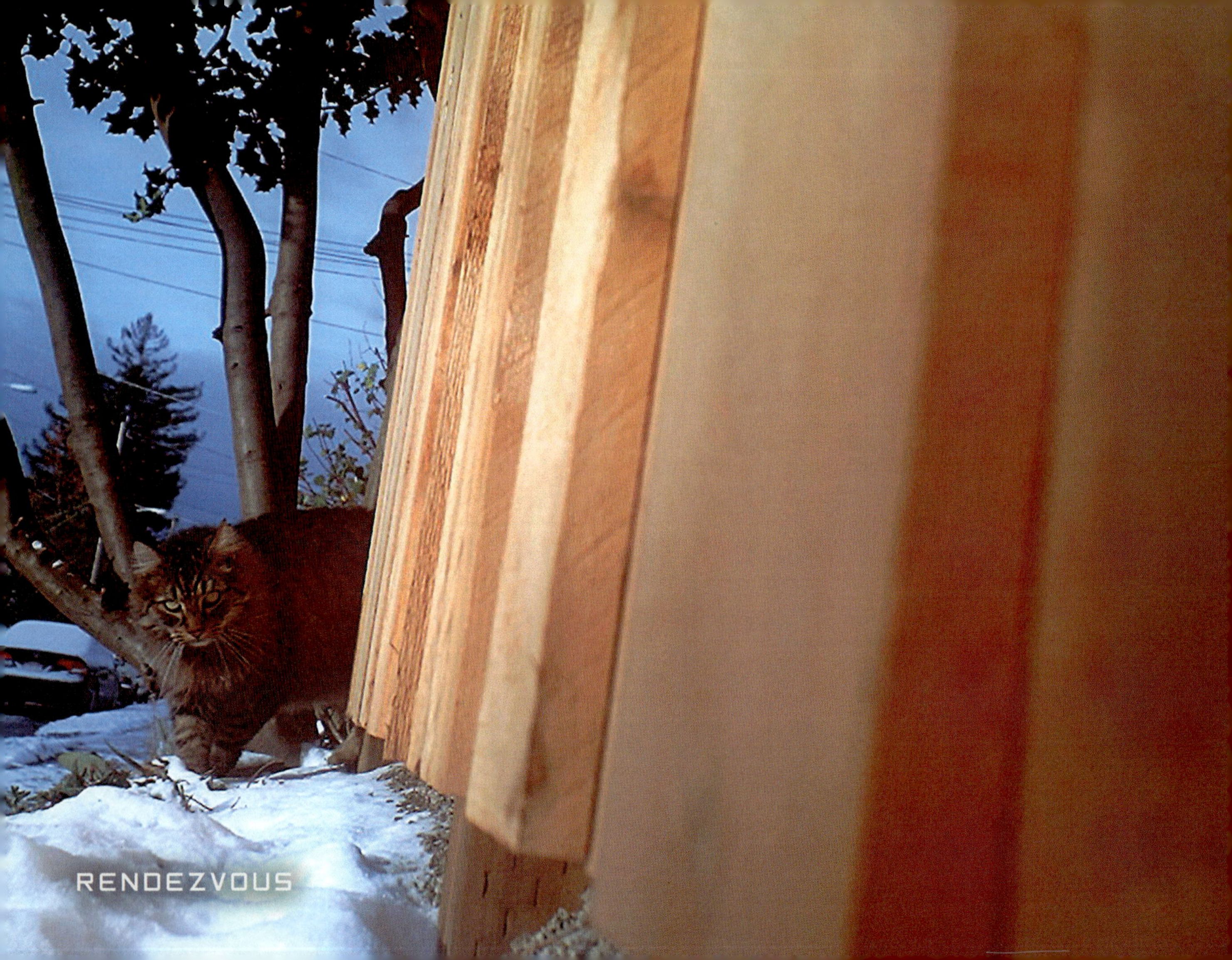
RENDEZVOUS

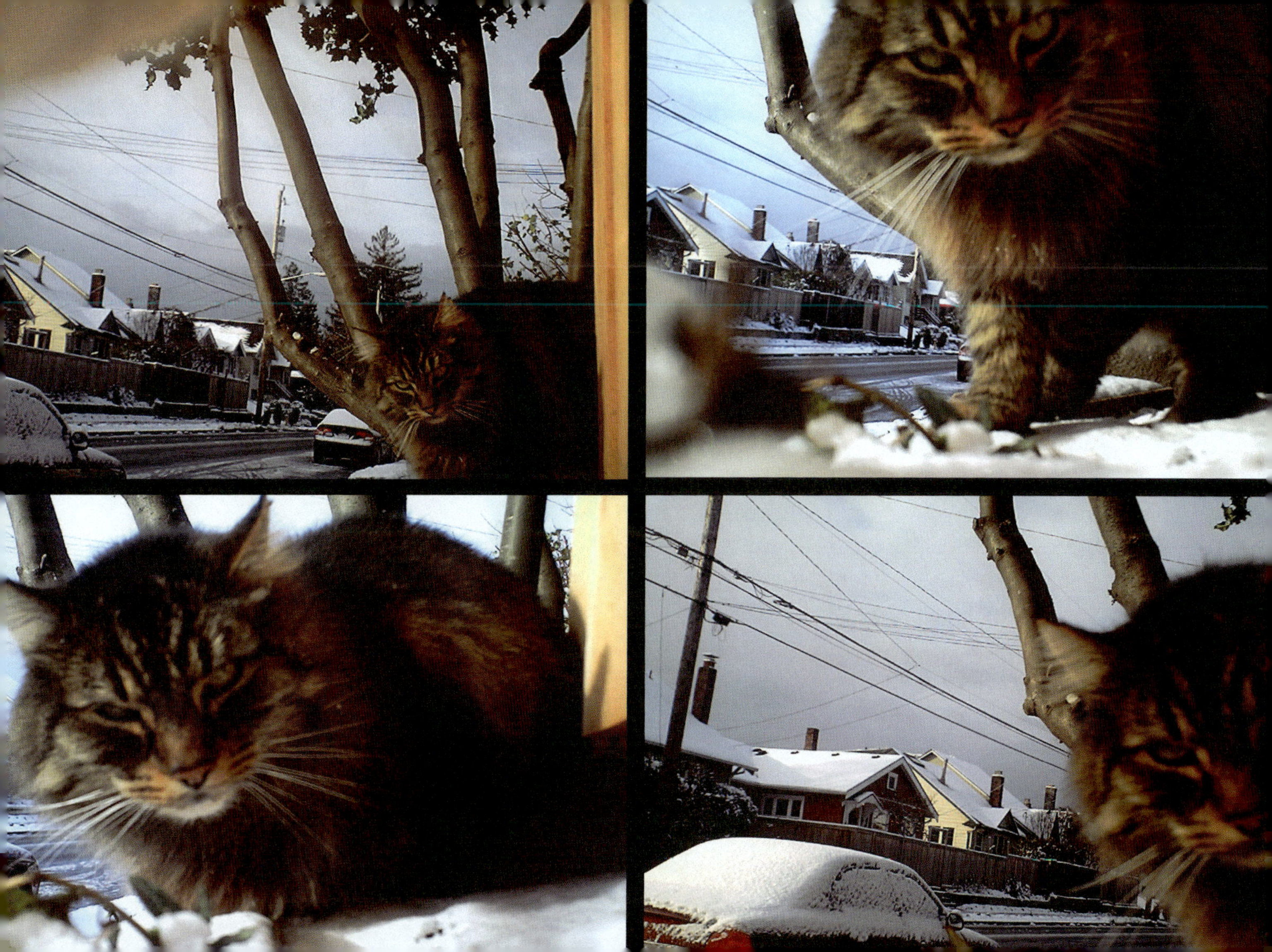

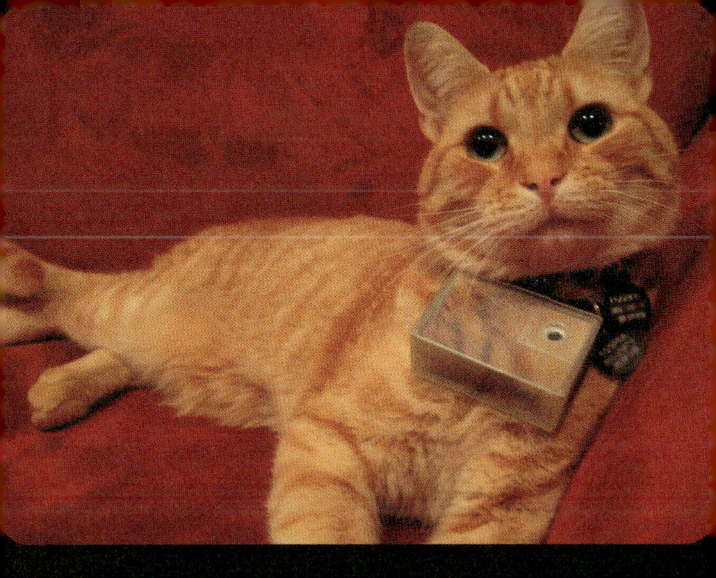

Cooper lives in Seattle with his family. His photos are never cropped, color corrected or manipulated. Follow his continuing adventures: www.PhotographerCat.com

This is Cooper's first book. A portion of proceeds is donated to PAWS: Progressive Animal Welfare Society

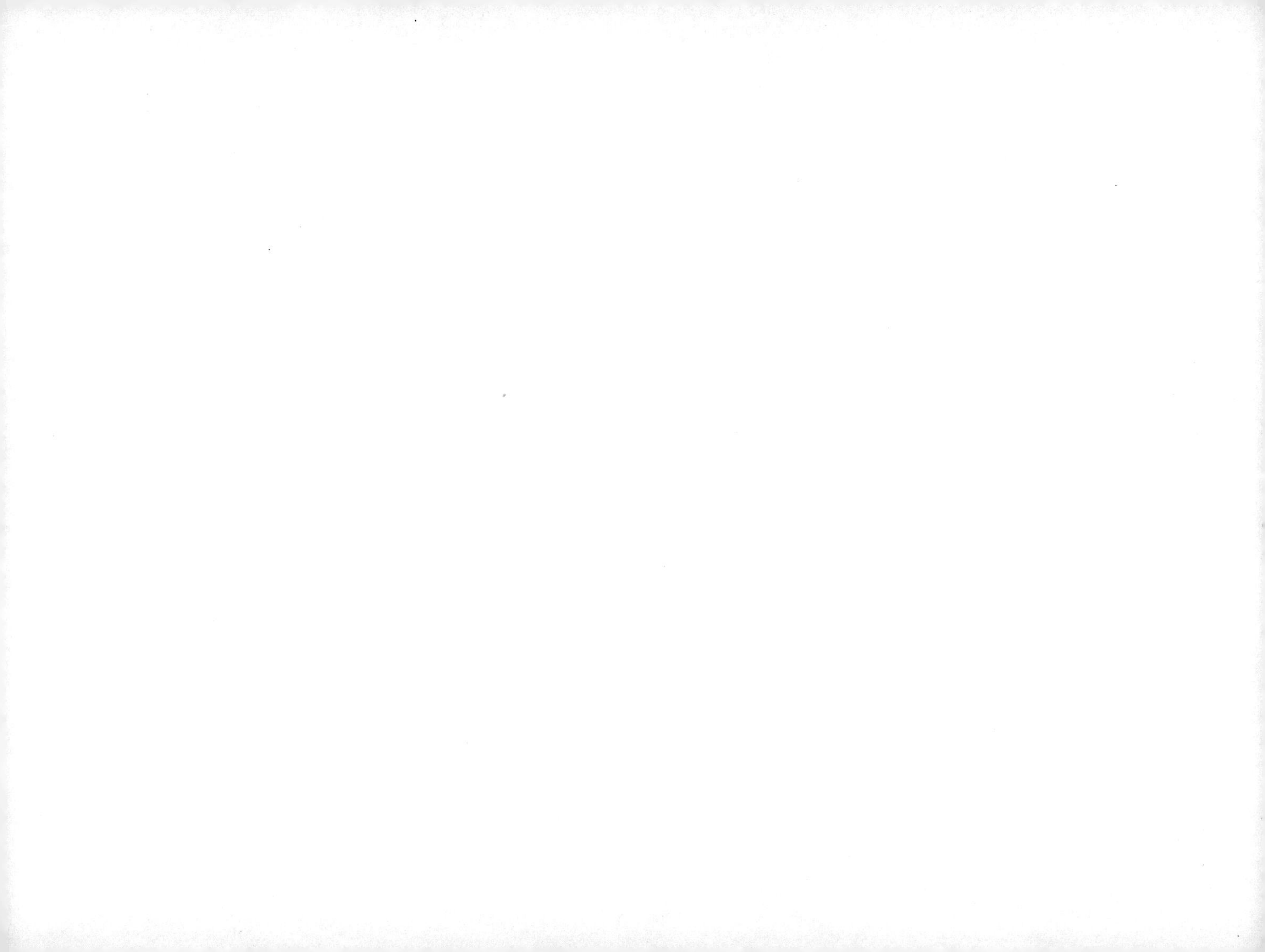

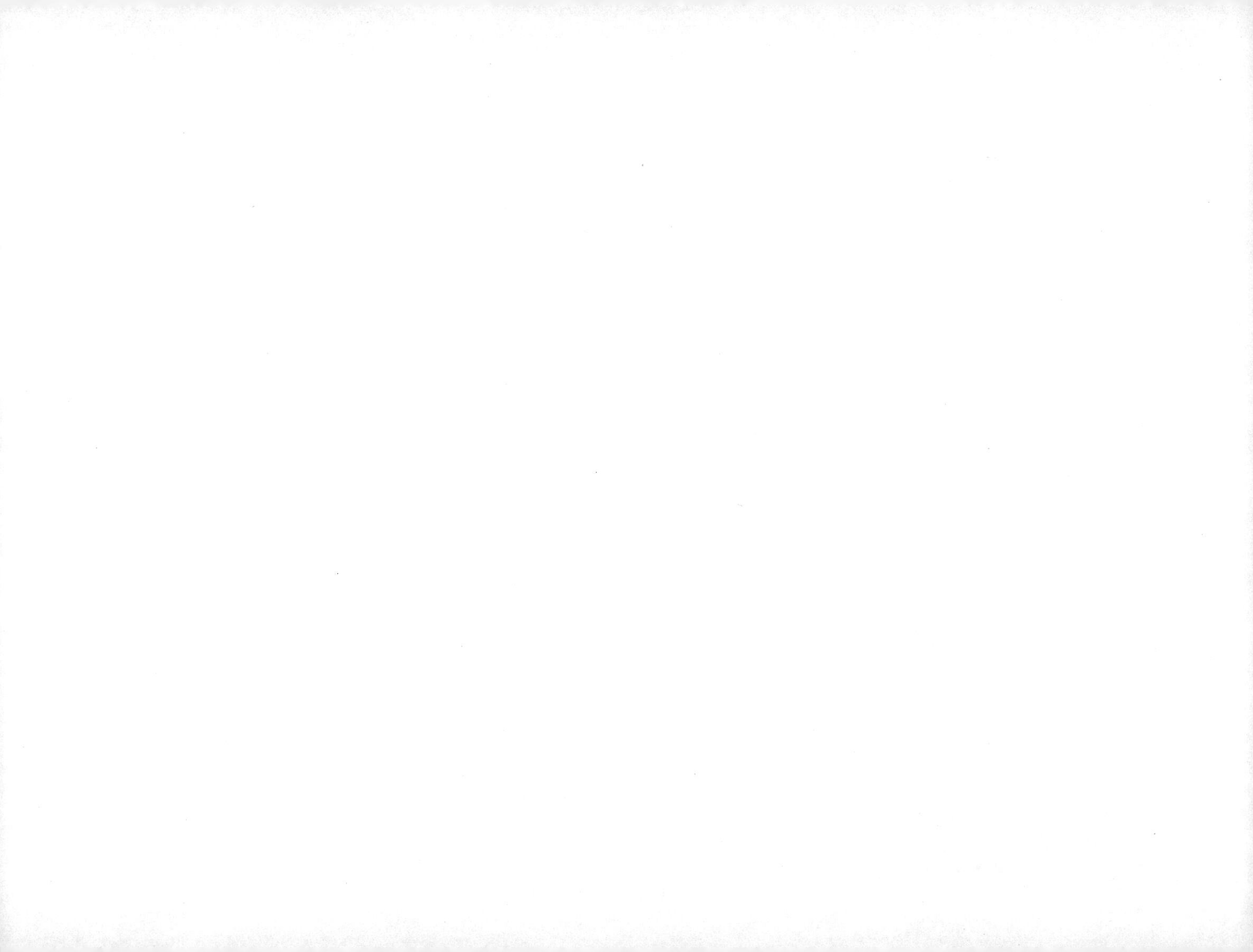

Printed in Great Britain
by Amazon.co.uk, Ltd.,
Marston Gate.